What People Are Saying About Steve's Reiki Attunement Programs

-After the wonderful experience I've had with your Reiki 1st Level Attunement I'm very much interested in obtaining the Reiki 2nd Level and Master programs. You have done such a powerful job on the Reiki 1st Level that I haven't any doubt that these tapes will be just as successful. Thank you again on behalf of myself and my kids. ***C. B.***

-Very powerful attunement. The attunement with the Master Symbol has increased my Reiki. My whole family notices the difference. I recommend this when you are ready. I have now taken all three attunement programs and am happy and pleased with all three. ***P. D.***

-My husband and I watched the video together and received the attunement. We both experienced the energy, but different things happened in our hands. His was a hot, smooth sensation and mine was hot and pulsing. He said the crystal became three dimensional (in the room) and glowed different colors for him. Thanks for making the film and please continue to make more. ***K.L.***

-I am a Reiki Master and use these programs for my students. Besides the wonderful attunements, they are very good for showing the Reiki Symbols and how to use them. These programs give you an option if you can't receive an attunement in person. ***D.D.***

-I tried this video because I had wanted to take a first level Reiki Attunement and couldn't afford the high price. This one gets better each time I do it and I can now give Reiki to my husband. We both see and feel results. This video is a true blessing to us all. ***O.R***

-I am very pleased and happy with attunement program. The Reiki symbols are very powerful and do help with my Reiki. Program makes it very easy to understand how to use them. I recommend this program when you are ready for 2nd Level Reiki and Symbols. ***G.A***

-I highly recommend this video to all those interested in being initiated into Reiki or strengthening their healing powers at the Reiki

1

1level. I was fortunate enough to be initiated by a local Reiki Master and at an affordable price but that was it - many of us are then on our own. Video can provide many invaluable 'booster' attunements. *J.L.*

-We purchased the whole series, Level One, Two, and Three. Your videos were even more of a powerful attunement than my local Reiki Master. Thank You! Looking forward to hearing from you. *K. S.*

-I absolutely loved the presentation and you did the best Reiki 2 presentation that I have ever attended. I was very impressed with the amount of information presented in the tapes. Thank you so much for the effort that you have put forth in this series. *C. W.*

- I can testify that these 'on-demand' distance attunements carry the same degree of power and potency that a face-to-face traditional attunement does - there is no doubt about it. In fact, this video provides a stronger energy flow through the hands than traditional Reiki 1. Everyone can afford to receive a genuine attunement & experience the life-enhancing wonder that is Reiki. *J.M*

I want to tell you how successful the tapes were in attuning me with Reiki. I have used it quite a bit already, especially on myself as I am going to have surgery tomorrow. Thank you. *D.S.*

I'd like to thank you very much for providing this wonderful way to receive attunements. I was able to feel the connection with you right away and actually saw movement swirling around me during the process and felt tingling and the sensation of being touched. My Reiki was immediately boosted after Reiki 1 and 2 and quite noticeably changed after the Master Attunement. Namaste. *D. E.*

-I felt the connection upon seeing Steve's image on tape. I was skeptical at first but no longer. My Reiki has increased and I'm happy with the programs. *Q.L.*

-I was already a 2nd level, but this attunement reinforced my Reiki. Plus it filled in the blanks for me in using the Long Distance Symbol. And it gave me tips for using the other two Reiki Symbols. *S.G.*

Reiki
The Ultimate Guide
Learn Sacred Symbols and Attunements
Plus Reiki Secrets You Should Know

Steve Murray

First Printing

_____

Body & Mind Productions

Reiki
The Ultimate Guide
Learn Sacred Symbols and Attunements
Plus Reiki Secrets You Should Know

Published by
Body & Mind Productions
820 Bow Creek Lane Las Vegas, NV 89134
Website: www.healingreiki.com
Email:bodymindheal@aol.com

First Printing November 2003

Library of Congress Cataloging-in-Publication Data
Murray, Steve
The Reiki Ultimate Guide: Learn Sacred Symbols and Attunements
Plus Reiki Secrets You Should Know
/ Murray, Steve – 1st ed.
Library of Congress Control Number 2003094177
ISBN # 0-9742569-1-9
Includes bibliographical references and index.
1. Reiki 2. New Age 3.Alternative Health
4. Self-Healing 5. Spiritual 6. Healing

Cover design: Jay Trujillo
Type design, production and photography: Gracie Garcia
Editor: Stacey Abbott
Drawings: Andrea Harward

Printed in U.S.A.

4

VIDEOS-DVDS-BOOKS

BOOKS BY STEVE MURRAY

Cancer Guided Imagery Program
For Radiation, Chemotherapy, Surgery,
And Recovery

Stop Eating Junk!
5 Minutes A Day-21 Day
Program

Reiki The Ultimate Guide
Learn Sacred Symbols and Attunements
Plus Reiki Secrets You Should Know

VIDEOS & DVDS BY STEVE MURRAY

Reiki Master Attunement
Become A Reiki Master

Reiki 2nd Level Attunement
Learn and Use the Reiki Sacred
Symbols

Reiki Healing Attunement
Heal Emotional-Mental Physical-
Spiritual Issues

Preparing Mentally & Emotionally
For Cancer Surgery
A Guided Imagery Program

Preparing Mentally & Emotionally
For Cancer Radiation
A Guided Imagery Program

Dissolving & Destroying Cancer Cells
A Guided Imagery Program

Reiki 1st Level Attunement
Give Healing Energy To Yourself
and Others

Reiki Psychic Attunement
Open and Expand Your Psychic
Abilities

Preparing Mentally & Emotionally
For Cancer Surgery
A Guided Imagery Program

Preparing Mentally & Emotionally
For Cancer Chemotherapy
A Guided Imagery Program

Preparing Mentally & Emotionally
For Cancer Recovery
A Guided Imagery Program

Pain Relief Subliminal Program
Let Your Unconscious Mind Do It!

Fear & Stress Relief Subliminal Program Let Your Unconscious Mind Do The Work!

30-Day Subliminal Weight Loss Program Let Your Unconscious Mind Do The Work!

30-Day Subliminal Stop Smoking Program Let Your Unconscious Mind Do The Work!

VIDEOS BY BODY & MIND PRODUCTION

Learning To Read The Tarot Intuitively

Learning To Read The Symbolism Of The Tarot

This Guide is Dedicated to

Peter L. Recchia
And
Claudia Masek
Who inspired and encouraged my Reiki Journey

FOREWARD

We live in a world that is constantly changing and not always as we would wish. In order to cope with these changes we are forced to look for new and "old" ways to handle everyday events. Reiki is one of the ways I use to give meaning to my life.

I have been blest to have known and serve as a mentor to Steve Murray for many years. He is dedicated to sharing Reiki with as many others as is possible. His ways may not be the methods preferred by some of the Reiki predecessors, but his integrity and honor are not to be questioned.

Reiki The Ultimate Guide Learn Sacred Symbols and Attunements Plus Reiki Secrets You Should Know, offers practical information and guidance that is difficult for new practitioners to grasp at the time of the attunement. We have all wished we could have taken clearer and better notes at a time when we are excited. Steve's book offers simple step-by-step directions to make practicing Reiki easier.

I wish to thank Steve for his book, and I am confident even Reiki "old hands" will find it useful.

Claudia Masek
Reiki Master

CONTENTS

Special note to the Reader

I strove to write a clear-cut, easy to read and understand Reiki Guide with information that you will be able to use in your Reiki journey. I feel I have accomplished that. If you discover some of my information differs from what you have been taught, it does not mean your teachings are wrong. Or for that matter that my teachings are right. I explain in the guide the reasons for the variations in Reiki teachings and beliefs. And I believe there is not a right or wrong way with Reiki. It is up to the individual Healer to decide what feels right or maybe wrong and what works for them in regards to Reiki. If I had any other belief, that would be judgmental, and a very important spiritual law is not to judge.

I also want to state this guide is not about or does it contain life histories of Dr. Mikao Usui or Hawayo Takata. I acknowledge their importance in the resurgence of Reiki in modern times. The majority of readers of this guide are fully aware of their stories. But, if you are new to Reiki and would like basic information on Reiki and the lives of these two important individuals, I have listed a few (there are many published) books that I have read in the bibliographical section at the end of the guide.

Any questions or comments, feel free to contact me at my web site www.healingreiki.com

Namaste

Steve Murray

Reiki Ideals

Just for today, I will let go of anger
Just for today, I will let go of worry
Just for today, I will give thanks for my many blessings
Just for today, I will do my work honestly
Just for today, I will be kind to my neighbor and every living thing

"Believe nothing, no matter where you read it, or who said it, no matter if I have said it, unless it agrees with your own reason and your own common sense."
-Buddha

Chapter One

Maverick Reiki Master

I believe at this very moment as you read this, our vibrations and energies are connected in the now. The now is the past, present and future all layered and existing simultaneously. In this now I am going to share with you my knowledge, experience, and beliefs about Reiki that took many years to acquire. Just take what you need from this guide. If you discover something that does not agree with your beliefs and/or teachings, leave it here.

This Guide Was Created for:

♦ The many thousands of students who have successfully received my Reiki Attunements including the Reiki Master Attunement from my programs on video and DVD, and who are now ready for additional knowledge and guidance.

♦ 1st and 2nd Level Reiki Healers who would like additional knowledge about Reiki and attunements.

♦ People who are not Reiki Healers, but would like information about the attunement process and Reiki Symbols before they receive Reiki and /or become a Reiki Healer.

♦ Reiki Masters who want to receive additional knowledge, compare their attunement process and learn how to give the powerful Reiki Psychic and Healing Attunements.

I believe this Reiki Guide, in the hands of the groups above, will be able to manifest my Reiki Mission Statement below.

My Reiki Mission Statement

To make Reiki knowledge, guidance and attunements available to everyone that seeks them. To make Reiki 1st, 2nd and Master Level Attunements affordable for everyone, so healing can be spread throughout the world.

The Reiki Guide

Many years ago, I read every Reiki book that came out until I had to stop. I could not keep up with all of the new books that were being published. I found that most of the books started to have the same content: the history of Reiki, hand positions, the healer's personal journey, basic Reiki information, stories on Reiki healings and miracles. Some books were interesting and informative and some were not. Nevertheless, the information I was seeking was either very limited or non-existent at the time.

At that time in my life, I could never find a book that addressed the questions and answers that I was seeking about Reiki. I wanted to know about the attunements and how they were done, how to protect myself with Reiki in a session and contact spirits with Reiki. Also, I was seeking guidance with the symbols, whether Reiki would still work if I drew the symbols wrong, and why other Reiki Healer's symbols were different. Of course I did eventually find all of my answers, but it took years and it came piecemeal from experience and other healers who where receptive to sharing information.

A few books did come close to revealing some of the information I was seeking. However, they always stopped short of divulging it. They always stated that the information was a secret and gave their reasons for keeping it a secret. These reasons never resonated well with me. Over the years it became my firm belief that the reasons for Reiki secrets were no longer valid, especially in this day and age. I will discuss the reasons supporting my beliefs later on.

For these reasons I made the vow, that if I ever wrote a Reiki book, it would be for people like myself. It would contain the information that I was unable to locate long ago.

Recently, publishers have approached me and tried to convince me to write a Reiki book. They contacted me due to the widespread notoriety and success of my Reiki

Attunement programs. I always declined because they wanted me to write the same type of book I stopped reading years ago.

The Journey Begins

I am going to keep my personal journey very short. Every person has success, failures, heartache, drama and challenges in their lives and I am no different. But, that could be a book in itself, and that is not what this guide is about. I will give you a brief overview of my journey only because I feel it is important for you to know how it was instrumental in writing this guide.

When I received my 1st Level and 2nd Level Reiki Attunement years ago, it changed my life. But, as I mentioned before I had a lot of questions about Reiki. My Reiki Master at the time would never really answer my questions to my satisfaction. I did get some stock answers, but when I really wanted answers about attunements, symbols, and additional Reiki information, I was always told it was secret and sacred. But, if I became a Reiki Master I would become enlightened, and would find everything that I was seeking.

That sounded like it was the answer to my search. Unfortunately, at that time the fee for becoming a Reiki Master was $10,000.00. Well to make a long story short, I did not have the money, but I was determined to acquire knowledge on Reiki and become a Master. I made a decision. I would become a Reiki Master, and I would make becoming a Reiki Master affordable and available to anybody that wanted to become one. Of course, I really did not know how that was going to happen. I was not even close to becoming a Reiki Master or having any real Reiki knowledge or experience. It was a promise I made to myself out of frustration.

I informed my Reiki Master that I was going to attend other Reiki groups, seek out other Reiki Masters for information and receive additional attunements. I was soon told in a heated conversation that if I went elsewhere, I could never come back to this Reiki Master or group. This really confused me, because the Reiki Master seemed very spiritual and the teachings reflected that. However kicking me out for seeking enlightenment elsewhere was very disturbing to me to say the least. Unfortunately, I learned through the ensuing years that there can be, at times, politics, fear, closed minds and even drama associated with Reiki Healers. I never let that discourage me because I understood that as human nature, and it can and does happen in all walks of life. I always made it a habit to look at the teachings, not the teacher. Then, I would only embrace the teachings that worked for me, and leave the rest.

As we all know everything happens for a reason, so I left the Reiki Master and group and started my personal journey with Reiki. It was a journey that took years, and travels around the country. I even ventured to China to learn about Reiki and healing. Sure, in my travels I did meet a few Reiki Masters that held the same beliefs as my first one. But, through the years I found many healers like myself, who were open minded, willing to embrace new ideas and change with Reiki. In fact, the majority of the new generation of

Reiki Healers are like that. They "talk the talk"and "walk the walk" when it comes to unconditional healing.

The Maverick

I was labeled a Maverick Reiki Master years back for the way I started passing the various types and levels of Reiki Attunements through video programs to people throughout the world. The method I used for these video programs, and still use today, does pass the Reiki Attunements successfully. There have been thousands of people who have received attunements this way and are now channeling Reiki. From the moment I first made the attunement programs available, they were well received, and still are. But the programs did upset and rock the beliefs of a few Reiki Masters around the country. They labeled me a Maverick Reiki Master, and sometimes a few other names. I will talk more about the reaction from this select group later on. However, ironically enough, Reiki Masters are now passing attunements the same way. Plus they are using the Internet, phone and of course long distance, successfully. Thus, I was labeled a Maverick years ago, for something that is now both common and accepted most of the time. The world is now full of Maverick Reiki Masters and Healers, so I am not alone anymore.

How the Attunement Programs Came to Pass

To make my Reiki Mission statement a reality, I knew I needed a way to pass Reiki Attunements to people around the world who did not have access to a Reiki

Master and/or did not have the funds for Reiki and Reiki Attunements.

That group included tens of thousands of people who were becoming aware of the healing power of Reiki through articles, books, internet, TV and word of mouth. I needed a medium to pass attunements to these people so Reiki could be made available to them.

I was actively sending Reiki into the past, present and future successfully (as many Reiki Healers do) with my intent and the Reiki Symbols, including the Long Distance Symbol. So I knew it was possible to have a universal medium to pass Reiki Attunements, but how?

In a dream the solution came to me. I would incorporate spiritual and metaphysical laws that I learned over the years into the attunement to make sure it was received. I would perform the attunements in a place that was a known source of natural energy and had an abundance of it. I planned to use the Reiki Symbols and my strong intent to channel the attunements into a large crystal. I would then combine all these elements into a video, which will serve as the medium for passing the attunements.

I soon set Reiki in motion to help in acquiring all the elements and find the people I needed to make the Reiki Attunement programs become a reality. Everything fell into place and three months later I was on the vortex called Bell Rock in Sedona, Arizona performing the first three Reiki Attunement video programs, the Reiki 1st Level, Reiki Psychic and Healing Attunement. It took all

21

day for me to prepare and do what I had to do to ensure the attunements would be passed and then film them. Not once were we disturbed on the vortex while I was doing the attunements. In fact, I recall only seeing a few people. The vortex was magically cleared for the day.

The Fallout From the Few

When these programs were first released, they gained a great deal of notoriety and popularity. Within the first month I started to receive hundreds of e-mails and letters from people thanking me for the programs and saying they received the various attunements and were now channeling Reiki. Many of the letters told about Reiki healings and miracles. But, I did start to receive some negative feedback from a few Reiki Masters. They had several issues with the programs that tied into their own beliefs, teachings and abilities. The funny thing is not one of them that wrote said they took the attunement. Nor did they take the time to see why and how I was passing the attunements. They always attacked me personally for what I was doing.

I had expected and was prepared for receiving comments like this, so it did not bother me or slow me down. I really did not produce the attunement programs for my opponents, it was for all the people who were taking the attunements and writing and thanking me for making Reiki available to them. My Reiki Mission Statement was beginning to manifest.

The few Reiki Masters that wrote always stated the same thing; you can only perform the attunement in person. My reply was always that maybe *they* cannot pass an attunement using a video as a medium, but I certainly can and do, along with other Reiki Masters that have the knowledge and ability. Then, I always asked, what about the people who have taken the attunements and claim they have received them? What about their statements acknowledging they now channel Reiki to themselves and others? Furthermore, what about their experiences with Reiki healing from these programs? Are these people mistaken or making it up? I always knew these people received the attunement, and they knew they received it, so as a third party they were passing judgment. In all spiritual paths including Reiki you are taught not to judge. Usually I never received a response after my reply. A few that did answer would acknowledge that maybe there is some truth in what I said and maybe there was room in the world for different Reiki beliefs.

I did receive an answer from one Reiki Master stating that maybe my reply was true, but these people were not getting healed and receiving Reiki the right way. That reply really baffled me–to say that after a person was healed, the way they achieved it was wrong–did not make sense. The only thing I could ascertain from this letter was if a person was healed through this Master's beliefs and teachings, then it was OK for them to be healed. Again, this Master was making a judgment on other individuals' healing.

If this small group of Reiki Masters had taken the time to see what I was doing and teaching, maybe they would have discovered they were teaching and doing the same thing. And I was not the only Reiki Master doing that, but perhaps just the most public. They also should have realized that my programs were not produced for everybody, just the students that were drawn to me.

My strong belief is all the Reiki Masters that contacted me had good intentions and strong beliefs about how Reiki should and should not be done, and I respected that. How they use and teach their Reiki is good for them, their path, and the students who are drawn to them. But, the way I was guided to do Reiki is good for my path and the students who are drawn to me. The bottom line is: this is a big world and there is plenty of room and a great need for all Reiki Healers regardless of their beliefs and teachings. All Reiki Healers and Masters should focus on the healing at hand (no pun intended) and not be judgmental of anything, most of all Reiki.

As time went on I very rarely received comments from Reiki Masters like I did at first. As I mentioned earlier, the new generation of Reiki Healers was fast evolving and shifting rapidly, with a higher level of awareness, openness, and acceptance to change. There were now thousands of Maverick Reiki Masters teaching and using Reiki. There are Reiki Masters now that even use my programs in their classes.

OK, that's enough of an overview of my journey and how the Reiki Guide came to be. Now I can move on to the rest of the guide to provide knowledge and guidance on Reiki.

"Every human being is the author of his own health or disease."

-Buddha

"Your work is to discover your world and then with all your heart give yourself to it."

-Buddha

Chapter Two

Reiki Guidance

Reiki originates from Japanese words. Reiki is pronounced *ray-key*. Reiki is made up of two words, **Rei** and **Ki**. The most common definition of **Rei** is *universal*. The most common definition of **Ki** is *life energy*. So, Reiki translated is Universal Life Force. There have been other interpretations of **Rei** which include Spiritual, God-Conscious, Higher-Self and they are all correct.

Reiki

Here's a metaphor for how Reiki works, though simplistic, it will illustrate the concept. When you are channeling (giving) Reiki you are like a powerful battery charger connected to an unlimited source of energy. You give this powerful charge to a person whose battery is low or drained for whatever reason; illness, stress etc. Once the person receives this charge, it goes where it is needed to help heal their circumstances.

I believe Reiki is our life force that keeps us alive. Once the life force is no longer flowing, our physical bodies cease to exist. This life force is called many other names in other cultures now and throughout the history of mankind. A few examples are: chi, manna, Holy Spirit and the list goes on.

When you receive Reiki and Reiki Attunements, they increase and help this life force flow without blockages through all your bodies (mental, physical, emotional, spiritual). This enables the bodies to be nourished by the life force, which enables them to become balanced and then healing can occur.

Reiki Level Attunements (1st, 2nd, Master) give you the ability to be a channel for this life force so you can give Reiki to yourself and others.

I believe everybody can naturally channel life force to a certain extent. There are even a few gifted natural healers that never received a Reiki Attunement, and are successful. But, Reiki Attunements are needed by most people to open and increase their natural abilities with this life force.

Reiki naturally enters your physical, mental, emotional and spiritual bodies in many ways. In your physical body, you breathe it in and it enters your Chakras. Reiki is needed in every living cell in the body and when it is low or cannot reach cells, imbalance ensues and illness will manifest.

Reiki also enters and flows into the energy field of the other bodies, the mental, emotional and spiritual. When Reiki enters these bodies it supplies the life force where it is needed so balance can occur, thus healing can manifest. Reiki has its own consciousness and goes where it is needed. It is the same consciousness that knows how and when to heal a cut or wound in our physical bodies.

When Reiki's flow is disrupted, blocked and or/slowed down, it creates an imbalance in the body (mental, spiritual, emotional, or physical) where it occurs. If the imbalance is not corrected, eventually the problem will resonate to the other bodies. For example, if you have an emotional situation (argument, divorce, financial, death etc.) that causes an imbalance in your emotional body and it is not cleared or released; the continued stress of this imbalance will resonate down to your physical body. This will ultimately weaken your immune system and your physical body will be affected ultimately with illness and disease.

The same can happen with your physical body. If you have a broken arm, and it is not set, your physical body becomes unbalanced, affecting your emotional and mental body. You would become short tempered and not able to think clearly because of the constant pain of the broken bone.

I have found the last place an illness or disease usually manifests is in the physical body. The reason is because most of the time the imbalance starts in the mental and emotional body. Negative emotions, feelings and thoughts can also cause blockages in the flow of Reiki. Keeping balance on all levels is the key to staying healthy on all levels. Reiki will help with this.

Channeling (giving) Reiki

Channeling Reiki is the same as giving Reiki. When giving Reiki you become connected to the source of it and you become a channel for this life force. It then will flow through you and out your Palm Chakras. Receiving a 1st, 2nd, or Master Level Reiki Attunement will enable you to connect to the unlimited source of Reiki and have it channel (flow) through you when you desire to channel it. The majority of the Reiki you channel flows from the source into the Crown Chakra and out your palms. But, some of it also flows in from your other Chakras and even from breathing in air. Reiki Healers channel Reiki to themselves or others with their palms on the body or a few inches off. The channeling of Reiki can also be done with beaming Reiki (explained in a later chapter).

Reiki Attunement

An attunement is a sacred process, initiation and/or meditation with a specific purpose or intent. The main purpose and intent of the Reiki 1st, 2nd, and Master Attunement is to connect (attune) you to the source of Reiki so it can flow through you when you need to channel it. During the 2nd and Master Attunements you are also attuned to the Reiki Symbols. In the Psychic and Healing Attunement the intent and purpose is to open your psychic abilities and promote healing. These last two attunements do not enable you to channel Reiki.

Reiki Session

A Reiki session (term I use) or a Reiki treatment is when a Reiki Healer channels Reiki to a person. I recommend never using the word *treatment* with Reiki because of the legal ramifications. A session is not an attunement. But, a Healing or Psychic Attunement could be part of a session. Psychic Surgery, Scanning and Beaming Reiki to a person can also be in a session.

Reiki sessions vary from Healer to Healer and it all depends on the needs and circumstances of the person receiving the Reiki. In a typical session I find out if the client is experiencing any pain in any area, then make a note to channel Reiki to it. I will channel Reiki to the seven Chakras for about a minute or so. Next, I do a quick scan over the body to see if there are any problem areas. If so, I will channel to those areas. Then, I will channel to the problem area that was mentioned at the beginning. But, each session is different and it all depends on the needs of the client which determine what I do during a session.

Chakras and Reiki

Chakras are key factors in all aspects of Reiki and you should at least have an overview of what they are. Chakra is a Sanskrit word meaning wheel, or vortex. When I refer to Chakras, I am talking about the energy centers located at portals throughout your physical body. There are seven major Chakras with other smaller ones that include your hands (palms) and feet. Chakras are areas (portals) where energy flows in and

31

circulates through your system. Energy can also flow out of Chakras in several ways. For example, you could have blockages that lead to energy loss through one of these portals. Or, you can be giving Reiki and it can be flowing out your Palm Chakras, which is what you desire.

When you are channeling Reiki, it flows into you through your Chakras. The majority of the Reiki I have found, flows into your Crown Chakra and Foot Chakras (soles) and flows out your Palm Chakras.

The goal for our health is strong, clear Chakras that are "spinning" open, bright and clean. When this is achieved our energy system is balanced. Balanced means energy is flowing smoothly and unblocked and can get to where it is needed for healing, building and nourishing the physical body.

When a Chakra becomes blocked from Psychic Debris, an imbalance occurs. If it is not cleared, it can have a domino effect on the other Chakras and that is when illness and disease can manifest. Reiki can very effectively clear these blockages.

The following are the Seven Major Chakras as I was taught. There are some differences in some teachings, but they all are fairly similar.

Seven Major Chakras

◆ First Chakra: also called the Root Chakra, is located at the base of the spine. It is linked to survival instincts and our ability to ground ourselves in the physical world.

♦ Second Chakra: located just beneath the navel. It is related to our sexual and reproductive capacity.

♦ Third Chakra: located behind the solar plexus, which gives us a sense of our personal power in the world.

♦ Fourth Chakra: also called the Heart Chakra, is located at the heart and gives us the ability to express love.

♦ Fifth Chakra: located in the throat, is linked to creativity and communication.

♦ Sixth Chakra: also called the third eye, is located between the eyebrows. This is the center of intuition and awareness.

♦ Seventh Chakra: also called the Crown Chakra, is located at the top of the head. This is related to one's personal and spiritual connection to the universe.

Four Bodies

I believe we have at least four bodies; physical, mental, emotional, and spiritual. Of course the physical body is the only one most of us can see, but the other three are energy fields that are layered on top of the physical body. There are other teachings that state we have many more energy bodies, and that might be true. But, I always work with these four, which are the most important for most people. When I refer to bodies throughout this guide, I am talking about these four.

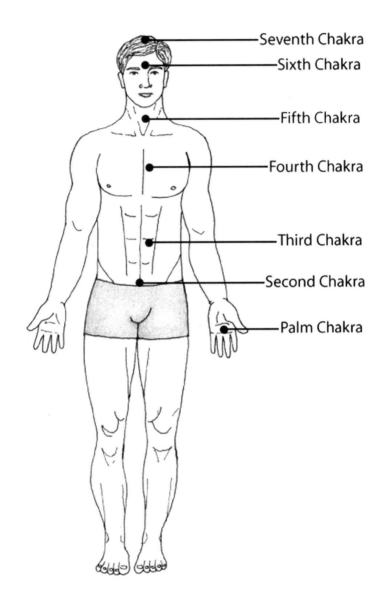

Seventh Chakra
Sixth Chakra
Fifth Chakra
Fourth Chakra
Third Chakra
Second Chakra
Palm Chakra

The Chakras

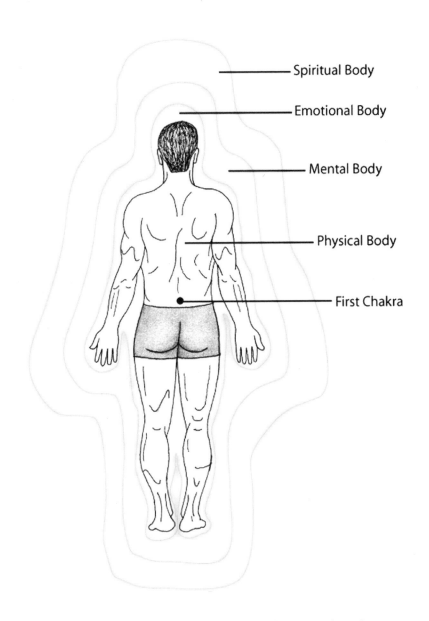

Spiritual Body

Emotional Body

Mental Body

Physical Body

First Chakra

The Four bodies: spiritual, emotional, mental and physical. Plus the 1st Chakra.

Psychic Debris

My belief is that people have physical health challenges for one main reason. It is that they relive past experiences from their lives over and over again in their minds. Unfortunately, most people still have a negative emotional charge connected to these past experiences. This emotional charge, whether it is anger, fear, anxiety etc., is experienced all over again, which creates what I call Psychic Debris. I am not saying it is detrimental to have the emotions at the time of the experience, they happen for a reason. Normally you experience the emotion, process it (understand the reason for it) and release it. It is when the emotion is not processed, understood and released in a timely matter that Psychic Debris occurs.

Psychic Debris eventually accumulates and creates blockages of your life force on all levels. But, this type of Psychic Debris starts in your mental and emotional body. If it is not taken care of, it will eventually affect your physical body and illness and disease will develop.

The secret to eliminating Psychic Debris is to relive or remember past experiences without the emotional charge connected to them. You should only remember the life lesson and understanding connected to the experience.

For example: I had a woman client who was very sick. She had a bitter divorce 20 years before and hated her ex-husband. The problem was she still relived the experience in her mind daily with the emotional charge of extreme hate attached to it. Each time she did this, her physical body experienced the anger all over again. She needed to release the emotional charge from this experience if she was ever going to heal. She was finally able to release the emotional charge of this experience (with the help of Reiki) and started to heal. No wonder her physical body became sick. She was experiencing extreme anger daily for 20 years.

The key to maximum health is when you have life experiences perceived as unhappy or negative, you go through the appropriate emotions connected with it and then release them. When you have a memory of the experience you will recall just the life lesson from it without the emotional charge.

For experiences in your life perceived as happy, loving and positive, you should keep the emotional charge. This type of emotional charge puts all your levels in a healing state. So when you relive and remember these life experiences you will be in a healing state. If my client had experienced an emotional charge of love, instead of daily anger for 20 years, most likely her physical problems would not have developed.

I understand releasing negative emotional charges is a difficult process that is not taught in school. But you will find as you go through your Reiki journey, it will become easier to let go of emotional charges and just take the understanding and learning from your life experiences.

The good news is that Reiki sessions and attunements help release and break up this debris where it is needed so you can understand and release the negative emotional charges. If it is in the physical body, you will feel and see the results quicker, even though healing is also happening on other levels.

When Psychic Debris in the mental or emotional body is released, you will develop clearer thinking, and a deeper understanding of thoughts, feelings and life circumstances. You will also be opened up to positive change. When blockages are released in your spiritual body, you will be able to reach a higher level of awareness and connection with your source. Once Psychic Debris is removed, the life force energy returns to its normal healthy flow. But, dealing with Psychic Debris is an on-going daily process. The life experience presents new challenges every day that must be worked with and released so new debris does not accumulate. Ideally once you are cleared, you continue to use Reiki to stay balanced and clear.

Intent

I cannot stress this enough - if you learn just one thing from this guide, let it be that when using Reiki your intent is very important. Your intent has to be clear and focused before you channel Reiki, give attunements, activate symbols, and/or send Reiki to the past, present or future. Anything you do with Reiki will be increased with strong intent.

Your intent is what the Reiki is going to be used for and/or sent to. Intent can be stated silently or out loud before you give Reiki, that is all that has to be done. You do not have to dwell on the intent once you start. In Reiki Attunements you must make your intent clear on which attunement you are going to give before you do it. For example, if you are going to give a Reiki Healing Attunement, you make your intent clear that it is a Healing Attunement before you give it.

In activating Reiki Symbols the key is your intent. Intend to activate them for what they are needed for, and they will. It is that simple once you are attuned to them.

It is taught by some Masters that Reiki will work without intent, that it is not needed. They even teach that you can just let your mind wander while doing Reiki. But, I believe if you want your Reiki to flow stronger and expand to higher levels, intent will do that. If you have been taught that intent will take care of itself or it is not important, try both ways, you will notice the difference.

Activating and Drawing Reiki Symbols

I receive a lot of mail from people around the world concerned about drawing the Reiki Symbols right and/or perfect for them to be activated and work. I am going to tell you now; the power of the Reiki Symbols does not come from drawing them perfectly. It comes from your intent to activate the symbol(s) once you have been attuned to them. So do not worry when you draw the symbols and they are not perfect, just draw them the best that you can. Make sure you draw the symbols the way you have been shown when you received your attunement.

Variations and Translation of the Symbols

Reiki practitioners and Masters on occasion, find out they have been attuned to and taught Usui Reiki Symbols that have different lines, extra lines, and lines that go in reverse directions.

There are a few reasons for the variations of the Reiki Symbols. In the past, Reiki Symbols were taught orally and students were not allowed to write them down for hundreds of years. So when it was time for them to teach the Reiki symbols, again, it was taught orally from memory. That not being the best system for accuracy, variations in the symbols did develop. Now Reiki Symbols are written down which keeps the variation to a minimum.

Another recent reason for the variations of the symbols, is that some Reiki Masters have intentionally changed the Reiki Symbols. They have done this to make their Reiki unique, personal and blend with their current beliefs, or they have been told by their Reiki guides to make the changes.

As for the translations and interpretations of the symbols, I have seen many different ones myself. But, I use the most traditional and accepted ones here in this book. Translations and interpretations are tough, especially when you go from several languages. The Bible is a prime example of that. It has been translated in many languages from its original. This has resulted in some discrepancies in some parts of the Bible and its translations.

Feel free to use an interpretation that you were taught and you feel comfortable with, just be aware and open to the different interpretations. There is no right or wrong concerning this. It is just a matter of who you received your information from. The important issue is the intent on the symbol's meaning.

Sending Reiki Without Permission

I believe you can send Reiki without permission especially to the past and future. There are some teachings that frown upon this. They want to seek permission for the Reiki to be requested before being sent. The challenge with this is there may be times when you want to help a person(s) who cannot be contacted. That person could be unconscious, traveling or lost. There are many circumstances when permission is difficult or impossible. You might have a person who needs Reiki and is not aware of it and is unapproachable.

When sending Reiki without permission here is what you do. Before you send it, state a prayer that includes your intent for the Reiki and ask the person to receive the Reiki only if it is for their highest good. If the Karma (destiny) is that the Reiki is not wanted and/or needed on any level, it will not be received and there will be no harm.

The Usui Reiki System

In the classic Usui System of Reiki there are three Reiki

41

Levels. There are three Reiki Attunements that correspond and are given with those levels. The levels are 1st, 2nd and Master. There are some Reiki Masters and schools that have four levels and attunements, which will be explained later on.

In the system of Classic Usui Reiki there are only four symbols used in Reiki and passing Reiki Attunements. There are other symbols that some Reiki Masters and schools are using and teaching, but they are not a part of the Classic Usui System. These symbols have been developed and created by different Reiki schools and Reiki Masters. They do have their own healing energy and uses. I myself have been attuned to some of these different symbols, and use them when they are needed.

The Reiki Master and Reiki Practitioner (1st and 2nd Level Reiki Healers) can use these symbols for specific purposes when using Reiki. This will be explained in the chapter on Reiki Symbols. The symbols available for use by the Reiki Practitioner depend on the Reiki Level they have been attuned to. The four Reiki Symbols are the Power, Long Distance, Mental/ Emotional and the Master Symbol.

In the 1st Level Reiki Attunement, the symbols are used in the attunement, but none are made available to the student. In the 2nd Level, the first three Reiki Symbols, the Power, Long Distance and the Mental/ Emotional Symbols are attuned to the student and the student can use them. The Master symbol is attuned and passed on to the student for use in the Reiki Master Attunement.

All the Reiki symbols are used in the process of giving all three Reiki Attunements.

Four Attunements

There are Reiki Masters and schools that use the Usui Reiki Symbols that have created a 4th Reiki Attunement. The 4th is an advanced attunement given after the 2nd Level Attunement. This attunement attunes a person to the Master Reiki energy and Master Symbol. The difference is they can use the Master Symbol and its energy, but there are steps left out of the attunement that enables them to perform and pass Reiki Level Attunements to students, clients, relatives and friends.

Important steps are left out in this attunement. Symbols are not placed in the Palm Chakras. The symbols need to be placed in the Palm Chakras to give the person the ability to give Reiki Attunements. You will be able to see what I am describing when you read the chapter and see the steps on giving a Reiki Master Attunement. The steps where I show the symbols being placed in the Palm Chakras, are not done in this advanced attunement. In my Reiki Master Attunement in person, on video and DVD, I do the full attunement. This gives the person the ability and option to pass Reiki Attunements if they desire.

Of course not everybody wants to be able to give Reiki Level Attunements or teach Reiki. So this fourth attunement is fine with them. There are two main reasons why this extra attunement was developed. Both were financial. Most students could not afford a full Master

Attunement, which passed the ability to give attunements because at the time this attunement was developed, it could cost up to $10,000.00. So the advanced attunement was developed so students could receive the Master Attunement and symbol for their own use at a reasonable fee. Also not having the full attunement passed, limits the Reiki Masters that can give attunements, which ensures a constant flow of students to these Masters.

Reiki Symbol's Origination

Reiki symbols are Japanese Kanji and are characters from the Japanese alphabet. The word Kanji is defined as "Chinese characters" and China is where Japanese Kanji originated. Kanji have characters that can have several different meanings depending on how they are used. This compares to the English language where words can have different meanings and uses in writing and speech.

Reiki Symbols have evolved over the years and have special meanings for Usui Reiki. Japanese Buddhists combined ancient Sanskrit with Japanese Kanji in their sacred writings and symbols so this most likely had an influence on the Reiki Symbols. The Long Distance Symbol and Master Symbol are accurate Japanese Kanji in their names and in the way they are drawn.

Usui Reiki symbols are not only used in Usui Reiki. This is the most widely held misconception taught about the symbols. They are used in different meditations and spiritual practices. For example, the Reiki Master Symbol is from Zen Buddhism.

Again, the Usui Reiki Symbols shown, explained and taught in this guide, are what has evolved and been derived from the Usui lineage over the years.

Reiki Symbol's Energy

Reiki Symbols are links to higher levels of awareness, manifestations and the source of Reiki. When you activate one, the energy with the specific intent of that symbol starts to flow. The Reiki Master Symbol is the ultimate symbol in this respect.

The Reiki Symbols without an attunement do not seem to be effective or have any power. They need the attunement that links them to the Reiki source and attaches energy to them. I believe you need an attunement for them to be effective and to work at their highest level. Without the attunement they are not connected to the Reiki source.

Reiki Lineage

A few Reiki Masters and schools put a lot of emphasis on Reiki lineage. I feel that this is not all that important, especially now with all the branches of Reiki that have surfaced. I do feel that there is confusion at times with the symbols used in the different lineages. There are Reiki symbols that are being called Usui, which are not Usui. That is not a problem if you have been attuned to these symbols, but you might like to know the Classic Usui Symbols. This guide will help you to compare your symbols if you have been previously attuned in a Reiki lineage. If your symbols are different, you might want to find a Master to attune you to the symbols in this guide.

The Attunement

I feel all attunements, if performed by a Reiki Master will be received by the student. The attunement can be in person, long distance Reiki, video program, phone, etc. Some people feel in person is the best and some people feel they receive stronger attunements from the other options. It really just depends on your needs, time and circumstances. It really should not matter how a person receives an attunement because it is an individual's decision.

When the attunement is given (it depends on what type of attunement) the Reiki Symbols are placed into your Crown, Heart and /or Palm Chakras. During attunements Chakras are opened and cleared. Reiki symbols are activated for use and there is a transference of Reiki energy during the attunement. Most importantly, you are connected to the source of Reiki.

What happens to a person during and after an attunement is very unique and can vary from person to person. It can be different each time you receive one. There is not a right or wrong regarding what you experience. It can range from an out of body experience, or visions to just a relaxed warm feeling all over.

After an Attunement

After a Reiki Level Attunement you will be shifting and processing Reiki (sometimes rapidly) on all levels; mentally, emotionally, spiritually and physically. This will create clearing and ultimately change, which will allow healing (balance) on these levels. Everybody progresses differently in terms of time regarding clearing and healing. You might not consciously sense or physically feel anything at first, but healing is taking place.

Ultimately you will start to sense and feel the change and healing on both a conscious and physical level. Unfortunately as I mentioned before, illness and disease usually occur first on the mental, emotional and spiritual levels. The last place it manifests is in the physical body. The same is true with healing, usually the last place it occurs is in the physical body, after the change, release and healing happens on the other levels. This means you can be healing and not sense or feel the results for awhile in the physical body. The good news is that Reiki works to speed up the healing process. You will also have more awareness of the healing as time goes on and you receive more Reiki and attunements.

Physical Signs of Reiki

Most people like to have physical signs to affirm that Reiki is flowing during Reiki Attunements and sessions. This includes the sender and receiver of Reiki. It seems to be human nature to want to have physical signs to wrap the conscious mind around, to confirm Reiki.

Reiki Practitioners, and even Reiki Masters are concerned about this. Most of the time there are indeed physical signs when using Reiki, but sometimes there are no physical signs. This does not mean the Reiki is not flowing, it is.

During sessions when there were minimal or no physical signs, ultimately the Reiki produced stronger effects after the session. The more you use Reiki, the more you become attuned to the Reiki energy and flow, and will always be able to sense when it is flowing. Reiki is a subtle, but powerful energy, when it flows into any body. It has to be this way to be used and absorbed. If it entered like a charge of electricity, there would be major problems with utilizing this life force on any and all bodies.

Some of the common physical sensations when giving Reiki are: warm to very hot hands, tingling sensations in hands or throughout body, hands cold to ice cold, numbness in hands and/or arms. You might experience a combination of sensations or have your own unique sensations. The person receiving the Reiki can feel the same physical sensations as above. Or at times you might not feel anything, but the person receiving it will, or vice versa. Usually both the sender and receiver will have physical signs. Each Reiki session can be different in terms of physical signs.

Emotional, Mental and Spiritual Signs

When a person is receiving or giving Reiki (this includes attunements), sometimes there can be other signs caused by Reiki flowing. The signs are caused by Reiki releasing blockages trapped and/or stored in the emotional, spiritual, mental and physical bodies. I refer to all these blockages as Psychic Debris, and they accumulate over time, which is not a good thing. These blockages must be cleared, so there can be balance throughout these levels, and then healing can occur.

As a result of this cleansing and releasing process various things might and can occur. You can have visions, flashes of insights, knowing of certain information, out of body experiences, colors experienced, music heard, different smells, or departed love ones and guides might appear. You could experience a combination of these, or just one.

A person might have an emotional release from Reiki, and start crying, nose start running and various fluids released from the physical body. This can happen at times from the release of old, deep emotional Psychic Debris that are blocked and/or trapped. Of course experiences like these do not happen during every Reiki session. The manifestations of these experiences are harmless and should not be feared. Just embrace it or at least accept it as part of a cleansing, releasing process that you must go through for healing.

Reiki Healing

Many healing miracles with Reiki have occurred and there are many books and articles that have documented this. But, usually Reiki is not a magic bullet. It's a healing modality that should be used in conjunction with other healing modalities to help heal and change your life. The types of healing modalities used with Reiki depend on your needs and circumstances.

For example, if you have a headache and use Reiki the headache goes away. But, the headache is from eating chocolate, and you eat it the next day and the headache returns. You will need another healing modality to help with the headaches. You then seek hypnotherapy to reprogram your unconscious mind to not eat chocolate. The Reiki helped in the short term, but the hypnotherapy helped long term.

If you are having surgery, you would use Reiki to heal quickly and be healthy before and after the surgery. If you need surgery, under no circumstances would you just use Reiki, and not have the surgery. Another example is that you have a broken bone. No matter how much Reiki is channeled to it, it will not set itself. You have go to the doctor and have it set, you then channel Reiki to it, and it heals faster.

Let me state this again, even when using Reiki, you still must do what you need to do in your life to change and heal. You have to do the work, be it diet, exercise, release work, getting medical treatment etc., Reiki usually cannot heal by itself.

You must have patience; you did not get into your situation over night. Regrettably it has taken a lot of people years to develop illness, and when they do, they want instant healing. Healing is a process and will take time and effort depending on you and your circumstances. For example: if a person needs to heal physically by letting go of 20 years of anger, they might heal slower than a person that needs to let go of only two years of anger. The reason being 20 years of anger has taken more of a toll on the physical body. But, there are exceptions and with Reiki anything is possible.

Sometimes even with the best medical treatment and

Reiki, the person does not heal physically and crosses over. Either it was too late for the physical body to recover, or it was the person's time to cross. I have found even in these situations, Reiki healing could happen on a mental, emotional or spiritual level. And when this happens this can even trigger healing within families and/or other circumstances and events.

Reiki Stops Flowing

I receive many inquiries from Reiki practitioners concerned that at certain times their Reiki has stopped flowing when they are channeling it. Do not worry, if you have been attuned I guarantee your Reiki is flowing. I did explain before what you can experience during Reiki. Just because you don't feel it physically does not mean it has stopped flowing.

Now, like all things in life, there can be an ebb and flow with the Reiki energy. At different times Reiki might flow with different intensities in a session or attunement, but that level of intensity is what is needed during that time.

Again, I know people are accustomed to a physical affirmation to prove something is working, but with Reiki at times there are very minimal, if any signs. Each Reiki session and Reiki Attunement stands on its own and is a unique experience. Once you are attuned to Reiki it is for life and it will always flow.

If you are concerned with this situation, just take a few Reiki Attunements for clearing and reinforcement, and you will soon have your physical signs back.

Time Between Attunements

I am repeatedly asked about how much time should lapse between taking the different levels of Reiki Attunements. Many Reiki Masters and schools have different beliefs, but ultimately I feel it depends on the individual and how they feel. The world and the people in it are evolving rapidly now, so less time is needed in between attunements. Yes, times have changed in regards to the old beliefs and the waiting time between the attunements.

Years ago it was said you should wait at least one to two years after you received the 1st Level Attunement, before you taking the 2nd Level. Then you wait three to ten years before you take the Master Attunement. And of course that would give you time to save for the $10,000.00 fee charged at that time. Even with that belief years ago, I took my 1st and 2nd Level Reiki Attunement on one weekend because I felt I needed both.

I feel the 2nd Level can be taken immediately after the 1st Level if you feel ready. The main reason is the 2nd Level does so much clearing and increases the flow of Reiki. It also attunes you to the three Reiki Symbols you can start using. These symbols really help take your Reiki to a higher level. Of course, if you feel you are not ready for the 2nd Level, you are not. Some people just have a 1st Level Reiki Attunement and they are content with that. They stay at the 1st Level all their lives.

It is common now for both the 1st and 2nd Level Attunements to be given during a weekend by Reiki Masters. Again I feel the 2nd Level taken right away, takes Reiki to a higher level. Plus the symbols are wonderful tools that give you so many options with Reiki.

Now for the Master Attunement, I believe you should take that when you feel ready. My only personal belief is that a Reiki Master should work with the Master Symbol and energy for at least six months before they start passing attunements. However, this is only my suggestion and belief. Do what you feel you are ready for.

Reiki and Healers

I believe all Healers use Reiki. It can be called other names, but ultimately it is the life source. Yes there are strong and gifted Healers that stand out and take healing to a higher level. As I stated before, some of these Healers have never been attuned to Reiki. But, sometimes they have been attuned from their cultures in a different method.

Sometimes it is taught that Reiki energy is special and unique from other energy. That is OK, and Reiki will work no matter what your belief. But, I believe there is only one life force that comes from our source no matter what you call it. I call it Reiki.

Reiki Can Never Cause Harm

I believe Reiki can never cause harm, because it is our life force. If it is the person's Karma (destiny) not to receive Reiki, they will not, but it will not harm them. Reiki can only heal.

Reiki and Contacting Spirits

Reiki can be used to help contact spirits when necessary. I devote a whole chapter to this towards the end of the guide.

Sage and Smudging

Throughout history many religious, healing, and spiritual groups have burned herbs for spiritual cleansing and purification. In Eastern cultures they burn incense in the temples and homes for the same reasons.

Sage is a sacred herb that has been used for hundreds of years among indigenous North Americans. They burn the sage in an energy cleansing and purifying ritual known as smudging. It is believed the smoke will attach itself to the negative energy and as the smoke clears, it is taken away and cleansed and the energy becomes pure and positive. Many healers now, including myself burn sage and smudge for cleansing and purification because it works so well.

I like to smudge with white sage which I purchase in smudge sticks. When you smudge yourself or another person, you start at the feet, and swirl (smudge) the smoke from the burning stick all the way up the body to the Crown Chakra. When you smudge a room or any area, you swirl the smoke in all the corners and

54

doorways. You can also draw the Reiki Symbols with the smoke from the burning stick when you are smudging for extra protection, cleansing and purification. You can smudge anywhere and anything including personal objects. The only challenge is sometimes smoke is not appropriate where you are so you cannot smudge.

Protection

Protecting yourself and others before, during and after a Reiki session and attunement is very important. I believe the Psychic Debris that is released during this time can become attached to you and/or stay in the room to become attached to somebody else or change circumstances. This is why you want to protect yourself and others.

There are several ways you can have protection, and many people develop their own way. Here is what I recommend and do myself.

Before any Reiki session or attunements you should do several things:

◆ Always wash hands before and after Reiki.

◆ Clear the room with the symbols you have been attuned to, by drawing them in all corners of the room. Some Masters suggest using only the Power Symbol for this, and that is OK. But, I feel you never know what is going to happen or be released, so it is better to be over protected than under protected.

♦ Draw the Reiki symbols you have been attuned to in front of yourself.

♦ Visualize or imagine white or golden light filling the area and surrounding you.

♦ You can sage the room and smudge yourself and your students or clients if you like.

♦ When you are through with the Reiki session or attunement, bring more white or golden light into the room and ask that any and all Psychic Debris be removed or dissolved now. Rub your hands together to break the connection with your client or student after stopping Reiki. Next quickly draw the symbols in the middle of the room and in front of yourself.

All of the above can be done rapidly and under a minute once you are experienced at it. That is unless you sage and smudge which will take a few minutes more.

Reiki Abilities

When you are looking for a Reiki Healer, look for one the same way you would look for any other professional. Talk to them first. Find out their beliefs and experience; speak to their previous clients and students. Find a Healer you feel comfortable with and trust.

Just like different levels of expertise and ability in any endeavor, not all Reiki Masters and Practitioners have the same level of ability and use the same teachings.

For example; one medical doctor will say a medical procedure is impossible because of his skills, ability and teachings. But another doctor will say it can be done because of his ability, skills and teachings and will perform the procedure successfully.

Who Can Be a Reiki Healer?

Anybody can become a Reiki Healer if they receive an attunement. You do not have to have a certain belief system, be spiritual or have a religion. Nor do you need to engage in elaborate studies of Reiki for it to work. But, you will find yourself seeking more information on Reiki and sharing experiences and techniques with other healers after becoming one yourself. You will find your life altered for the best, and usually will develop a higher level of consciousness and spirituality.

Uses for Reiki

I am going to make this simple. Reiki can be used for *everything* and *anything* that needs healing. That can be physical, mental, spiritual or emotional; past, present and the future. You can and should use your intuition for using Reiki.

With health issues, Reiki should be used in conjunction with professional medical treatment. Reiki helps all medical treatments and therapy.

Change = Healing

I believe that everybody has self-knowledge of what they need to do in their life. The challenge is that most

57

of the time it's buried in the unconscious mind. I believe that Reiki can help bring up this information so the person can receive and understand it. Then with this new clarity, they can make the changes and adjustments in their lives that need to be made. This can be a release of past events or people, changing life style, beliefs, habits etc. or a combination of them. The person of course has to be ready to know and accept this information, and everybody is on his or her own healing timeline. But, by the time the person discovers Reiki, they are ready for the process of change.

Change facilitates healing and my belief is that change is healing. Change for the positive-the way you eat, think, feel, exercise etc.-and you will begin to heal on all levels. Unfortunately, the hardest thing for most people is change in any aspect of their lives. Again, Reiki will help with this process of change.

Length of Reiki Sessions

I am often asked, how long should a Reiki session last? There are books and teachings that give certain guidelines for length of Reiki sessions, and instructions on where to start and end. They also give basic instructions for certain ailments. I personally find the prescribed length of the sessions, 45 minutes to and hour and a half, to be too long.

I believe once a Reiki healer becomes experienced with the energy and its flow, and the symbols are used, a session should never last longer than half an hour. Of course there are always exceptions to this and you will know intuitively when a session needs to be longer.

If you ask the person what they need to work on, and do a quick scan to find other areas that might need Reiki, then use the right symbol(s), plenty of Reiki will be channeled in half an hour or less. The bottom line is each session is different and you have to decide for yourself. But I feel that a session rarely needs to go for longer than 40 minutes for enough Reiki to be channeled.

Reiki and Animals

Yes Reiki can be used on animals and pets the same way as with people. Usually you do more scanning and beaming (explained in a later chapter) with them. With animals the length of a Reiki session is shorter, maybe 10-15 minutes.

Reiki Secrets

There is a belief with some Reiki schools and Masters that Reiki Symbols and Attunements, and the whole process should be kept secret. That is until there is an energy exchange, which is usually money, and then the secrets are told and taught. Then the person is instructed to keep these secrets for various reasons including the Reiki tradition.

I do not believe in this. Traditions do evolve and need to change with the times. I believe if a person seeks information about anything, including Reiki, they should be informed.

Now this does not mean I believe in free Reiki classes, sessions and/or attunements. It means I do not believe in secrets for any reasons, including control. I also believe this secret mentality has hurt the spread of Reiki and kept it from many people in need of it.

It has been said if a person sees the symbols, and knows about the attunement that negative energy can be created. And when the person does decide to try Reiki it will not work or be as strong. I believe this is all nonsense; the life force does not work that way. A Reiki Healer or a person contemplating becoming a Reiki Healer, or having a Reiki session should be fully informed, if they want to be. Of course, some people do not care about the process or how it works, just that it does. Reiki will work, informed or not.

Over the years I have been told other reasons for keeping Reiki secrets, but none have ever made sense to me, especially in this day and age. What does stand out in my mind is, with some Reiki Masters the secrecy is a control issue and some Reiki groups are like a cult with the information. Only a select few have it. And the reality is now most of the information is out there (most of the time incorrect) piecemeal via the internet, newsletters, word of mouth, books and even a few songs.

The metaphor I use for this is, say you would like and/or need a medical procedure. You want to obtain more information about the process before you experience it. But, the doctor does not want to tell you anything about it until it is done, then wants you to keep it a secret. Depending on the level of the procedure it could be kept a secret until you become a doctor. I have been told this is not a valid comparison, but in my mind it is. The only difference is the medical doctor does invasive procedures to your physical body. A Reiki healer works with all your bodies, thus all the more reason to be informed.

The new generation of Reiki Healers desire to be informed and share Reiki information with others. This will make Reiki more accessible to people throughout the world, which I believe is what it is all about.

Attuning Yourself to the Five Attunements

You can attune yourself if you are a Master, but I suggest the best way is to have another Master do it. What I am talking about are the three Reiki Level Attunements and the Psychic and Healing Attunements. It is my opinion that giving one of these five attunements to yourself, is like a lawyer trying to defend himself at trial, or a doctor operating on himself during surgery. Both can do everything associated with their profession for themselves well, except the two big items, trial and surgery. Reiki Masters are the same. They can balance themselves with Reiki and channel Reiki to themselves and others. They can give attunements, but when it comes to giving the five attunements to themselves, I recommend having another Master do it. Why would a Master need a 1st, 2nd, or Master Level Attunement again since they last for life? The answer is for reinforcement and clearing of the Chakras. I also mentioned earlier that this would help if the Reiki flow seems to diminish or stop. If possible, I suggest that all Reiki Masters receive reinforcement attunements every so often.

Reiki and Focus

I am always asked what to do when giving Reiki. What I suggest and do, is clear my mind of all thoughts. Then I focus my intent on what the Reiki is needed for and where it is being channeled. I soon become enmeshed in the feeling and flow of the Reiki and enter into what I would call an altered state. Soon my focus and flow of Reiki becomes one. During this period I try not to speak. Other Masters believe that you do not have to do anything special and can even talk when giving Reiki. That is OK if that works for you. But, I feel being focused during a Reiki session will increase the positive results of Reiki.

Clearing and Grounding with Reiki

When I use the word grounding I mean to connect and become at one with the Earth and your surroundings. Clearing means to clear and release blockages and Psychic Debris that have accumulated in your various bodies.

To clear and ground yourself with Reiki is a very simple, but powerful process to do and only takes a few minutes. I try and do it once a day in the morning.

You can do it anytime throughout the day when you feel the need. There are two ways I do it depending on my circumstances, though I prefer the first method.

1. I draw the four Reiki Symbols (three if you are a 2nd Level and none if you are a 1st Level) into both my Palm Chakras, then place both my palms over the 7th, 5th, 4th, 3rd and 2nd Chakras. For the other two Chakras I place my left palm on my 6th and put my right palm behind my back on the 1st and do both at the same time. I usually keep each Chakra covered for about 30 to 60 seconds. Sometimes I feel the need to keep them covered longer.

2. The second way is to visualize the symbols going into the Chakras, and focus on each one after the symbols go in for 30 to 60 seconds. This method is good if you are in a public place and need to be grounded or cleared, and do not want to draw attention to yourself.

If you are a 1st Level Reiki Practitioner, you would do the methods without the symbols. If you are a 2nd Level Reiki Practitioner, you use the three symbols.

"Peace comes from within. Do not seek it without."
-Buddha

Chapter Three

Reiki Symbols

Symbol Variations

If you discover that your Reiki Symbols have variations from the ones in this book, do not worry about it; you still received a Reiki Attunement. The symbols that you received from your Reiki Master are the right symbols for you to use because you have been attuned to them. What is important is drawing and using the Reiki Symbols you have been attuned to. Earlier in the guide I explained the reasons for the variations in the symbols.

The Reiki Symbols that I show and use in this guide are the Classic Usui Symbols that are the most true from the Usui lineage. There are really minor variations with these Reiki Symbols when they are traced back from this lineage. If your Reiki Symbols are different, and you feel you would like to be attuned to the Usui Reiki

Symbols in this guide, use my programs, a Reiki school or Reiki Master that attunes with these symbols.

Four Usui Reiki Symbols

The following are the four Usui Reiki symbols used in the Reiki Attunements and Reiki sessions. I will give their descriptions and a number of ways to activate and use them.

Reiki symbols do have their own energy and/or consciousness, and you can intuitively use them in different ways. You can use the following examples as a guide, but you can experiment with the symbols and become aware of many more ways to use them. I feel there is not a correct or incorrect way to use or activate these symbols as long as the intent is there. It is what you intuitively feel is right for you. As time goes on with your use of the symbols you will develop the techniques that work best for you.

Drawing the Symbols

When I say drawing the symbols, in Reiki that means tracing the symbols in the air with your fingers or eyes or visualize drawing them in your mind. The method you use to draw the symbols does not make a difference, and it might depend on your circumstances. If you are with a group of people and you need to draw the Power Symbol for protection, it might be a challenge to draw it in the air, so you would visualize drawing it in front of you. Some people have learned to draw the symbols without drawing attention to themselves. It is good to be versatile in drawing the symbols.

Cho Ku Rei

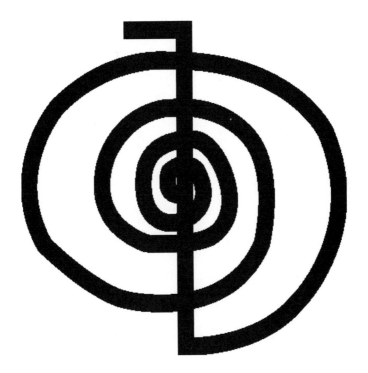

Power Increase Symbol

This is the Usui Power Increase Symbol. It is named the *Cho Ku Rei*. The name of the power symbol means, "Put all the power in the universe here."

The Power Symbol is used to increase the power of Reiki or to focus Reiki on a specific location. If at any time you want to increase the strength of Reiki you are giving, activate the symbol. The Power Symbol can be used anytime while giving Reiki. It is especially effective if activated at the beginning of Reiki to increase the power and at the end to seal in the healing energies of Reiki. I feel once you are attuned to this symbol, you activate it every time you channel Reiki.

The Power Symbol can also be used for protection from *anything*. When used for protection it is drawn around or in the area you want to protect. This can be a car, home, room, a person or yourself.

For example:

♦ Draw it around a car before you get in

♦ Draw it around yourself before giving Reiki

♦ Draw it around yourself before entering a meeting

♦ Draw it around a plane before flying

♦ Draw it around a boat before sailing

♦ Draw it around your children as they leave for school

♦ Draw it in a room you are in with negative energy

The above are just a few samples of how you can use the Power Symbol for protection. Use your intuition, imagination, experience and creativity for other protective uses for the Power Symbol.

Sei He Ki

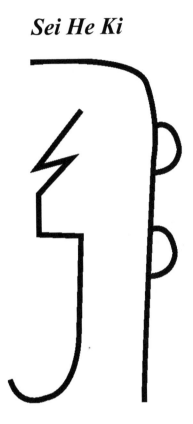

The Mental / Emotional

This is the Usui Mental/Emotional Symbol. It is also called the Emotional/Mental Symbol, Mental Symbol or the Mental/Emotional/Addiction Symbol. It is named *Sei He Ki*.

The name of this symbol means, "God and humanity become One." This symbol is used in emotional, mental and addictive healing. It balances you by removing and clearing any mental, emotional and addictive blockages.

This symbol is especially useful for healing relationship challenges. It can be used for any sort of mental and emotional situations. It can help stress, nervousness, fear, depression, anger, sadness and even your memory. The symbol can be used to help heal addictions as well as problems with weight loss, gambling and smoking. It can be used to help change or eliminate any unwanted habits.

A great way to use this symbol for yourself is to write your name on a piece of paper with the symbol or use your photo with the symbol drawn on it. Then hold the paper or photo between your hands while treating it with Reiki and at the same time hold what you need to heal in your mind. This will send Reiki to the parts of your mind and emotions that relate to your situation and will begin healing them.

When using this symbol, you activate it with your intent for its use at the start of a Reiki session. For example: if a client is depressed, the intent would be to help with the depression.

Hon Sha Ze Sho Nen

Long Distance Symbol

This is the Usui Long Distance symbol. It is also called the Long Distant and the Absentee Symbol. It is named *Hon Sha Ze Sho Nen*.

The name of this symbol has been interpreted a few different ways. I was taught it means, "May the Buddha in me connect to the Buddha in you to promote harmony and peace."

71

The symbol is very powerful and flexible. When activated with specific intent, Reiki can be sent anywhere, anytime in the past, present or future. It does this by connecting space and time with people, places, circumstances and events.

Again, with the Long Distance symbol you can send Reiki across the room or any location in the country or the world. Distance, time and space are not a barrier when you use this symbol.

Here are just a few ways to use the Long Distance Symbol in sending Reiki. Have a picture of the person you want to send Reiki to. This can be a person in the past, present or future. You may want to send Reiki to the past because you want to heal a certain relationship with someone. If that were the case you would draw the *Sei He Ki* symbol also. A reason to send Reiki in the future would be to a person having an operation in several weeks. The Reiki would be there for the person when they have the operation.

To send Reiki for the above reasons, place the person's picture in front of you and draw the Power Symbol then the Long Distance Symbol in the air or over it. You can also hold the picture if you like. Then start sending Reiki.

Or you can just write the person's name on a piece of paper, draw the symbols and hold the paper between your hands, then send Reiki. The whole process usually only takes five to ten minutes. You can tell when you are done because you will feel the Reiki stop flowing.

It you had a personal experience in the past you would like to heal and you know the approximate date, you can use the Distance Symbol to send Reiki back to heal the experience. It often helps if you have a picture of yourself close to the time the experience occurred. If you don't know the date and don't have a picture, it will still work simply by naming or writing down the problem and using Reiki. This technique can also be used for new or old problems that stem from past lives.

Let's go over in detail what you can activate the Long Distance Symbol for:

◆ Sending Reiki into the future for meetings, job interviews, operations, travel, and family gatherings. You can send Reiki into the future to any person, place or circumstance. Then the Reiki will already be there when you need it.

◆ Sending Reiki anywhere for any reason to a person, place or circumstance in the present.

◆ Sending Reiki into the past to persons, places and circumstances. Very few Reiki practitioners and Masters utilize this symbol for this purpose. But, it is a very important aspect of this symbol. My belief is the past, present, and future exist at the same time. They are in fact layered together. For example: if you send Reiki back to a disagreement with a family member that happened several years ago, the Reiki will create a

73

rippling, healing effect all the way to the present. The emotional charge or blockage created by the argument will be cleared. A shift will happen (healing) and the dynamics caused by the emotional blockages will start to change. You would soon find the relationship damaged by the argument with the family member start to heal.

The most common way this symbol is used is for the present, but it has just as many uses for the past and future. Use your intuition, experience and your needs and circumstances to guide you on using the Long Distance Symbol. Do not have fear in using and experimenting with it, you will be amazed at the results.

Dai Koo Myo

Usui Master Symbol

This is the Reiki Usui Master Symbol. It is named *Dai Koo Myo*. With this symbol there also have been several translations, but the one I use and was taught is, "Great being of the universe shine on me, be my friend."

The Master Symbol is the ultimate Reiki Symbol in all aspects. If you are a Reiki Master you will activate this symbol every time you use Reiki. It intensifies Reiki, takes it to a higher level and frequency and creates a stronger connection with your source. When you activate other Reiki Symbols with the Master Symbol, these symbols are then taken to their highest level of effectiveness. The symbol takes your healing abilities to the highest level you are capable of and expands your awareness and consciousness to greater levels.

Once you are attuned to the Master Symbol, you activate it every time you use Reiki.

Activating Reiki Symbols

When you activate a Reiki Symbol, it means you turn it on, make it work, go into action, etc.

There are several ways to activate the symbols and it depends on which way works the best for you.

I explained at the beginning of the chapter about drawing Reiki Symbols. Once you are attuned to the symbols, draw them the way you were taught and with intent and they will be activated.

You can activate a symbol by thinking of its name, or by saying it out loud if no one is around or silently if non-attuned Reiki people are present. You can visualize the symbol or imagine yourself drawing it or you can actually draw it to activate. Always use any way you feel intuitively to activate the symbols. I have just given you a few suggestions. From my experience there is not one right or wrong way for activating the symbols, it is what works best for you. Again, the most important factor is your intention in activating the symbols. Intend to activate the symbols and they will activate. You do not need to be in an altered state for the symbols to work. The symbols will do what they are activated for automatically.

How I Activate and Use the Symbols

Students always like to know how I personally activate the symbols. I always activate the Master symbol first when I use Reiki (of course I have been attuned to this symbol). If I'm using the other symbols I activate them next. The next symbol then depends on my intent or need for the Reiki. I always use the Reiki Master and Power Symbol at the end of each session for sealing in the Reiki.

I activate the symbols by drawing them mentally or physically three times on the palms of my hands. Next I say the name of the symbol silently and then I state my intent of the Reiki silently. If I do not have the time to do this or there are non-Reiki attuned people present, I will draw the symbols mentally and repeat them three times silently. Now if I am protecting a person, place, or thing I use the guidelines that I suggested in the segment about the Power Symbol.

I still experiment and use my intuition in activating and using the symbols. Since times and circumstances are ever changing, flexibility and creativity are keys to activating the Reiki Symbols. The symbols are powerful healing tools that you will find many uses for.

"It is better to travel well than to arrive."
-Buddha

Chapter Four

Preparation for Attunements

Attunement – a sacred process, initiation and or meditation with a specific purpose or intent.

The Usui System of Attunements

In the Usui Reiki System the 1st Level Attunement has four separate attunements. The 2nd Level Reiki has only one attunement, as does the Reiki Master Attunement. As I explained before there is not an advanced attunement in the Usui Reiki System. The major difference in the Usui Reiki Attunement system compared with other Reiki Attunements available, is that the symbols are placed in the third eye, which I feel is very important and powerful.

The three Usui Reiki Level Attunements are different in respect to what symbols are placed into the hands and third eye. This is when the hands are held over the head in a prayer position and the palms are held opened in front of the Heart Chakra.

During the 1st Level Reiki Attunement, only the Power Symbol is placed into the hands. During the 2nd Level Reiki Attunement the Power Symbol, Long Distance Symbol and the Mental/Emotional Symbol are placed into the hands. During the Master Attunement, all four symbols are placed into the hands.

Intention

Intention is most important in passing a Reiki Attunement and I cannot emphasize this enough. This is why I recommend you saying the type of attunement in a prayer, or state it silently in your mind at the beginning of any attunement you are going to give. This will also let your source be aware of the intentions of the attunement so it can be manifested and received. The Reiki Attunement will then be passed on to the student(s) during the process.

What to Expect When Giving or Receiving an Attunement

When giving or receiving a Reiki Attunement you can have many different experiences as explained in chapter two, but they are worth repeating because people are really concerned with this. You might sense or feel heat, tingling sensations in your hands and different parts of your body. You might see and feel colors, have visions, hear music or voices. You might simply have a nice warm feeling from head to toe. Everybody will have his or her own individual experience. There is not a right or wrong experience. You might have a different experience each time you give or take a Reiki Attunement. Or it might be just a subtle shift to a profound shift in your awareness. Do not have any fear, just go with the flow and understand the experience as part of the process. It is opening you up to higher levels of consciousness. And if you do not have any experiences as mentioned, you still received the attunement if the intent was there.

What Happens During an Attunement?

With the 1st Level Attunement you are connected to the source of Reiki, Chakras are opened and cleared, and so Reiki can flow through them. It means you are now able to channel Reiki to yourself and others when desired. With the 2nd Level and Master Level, the various symbols are placed into your Chakras so you will be able to activate and use them. With these two attunements your Reiki energy and flow is also taken to higher vibrations and levels.

Prepare for an Attunement

When passing a Reiki Attunement the Master must give the student(s) instructions on what to do while it is being performed. They will have their eyes closed and their hands will be guided into several positions during the attunement. I personally do not care if the student's eyes are open or closed. I do perform open eye attunements. Some students feel more comfortable with their eyes open. If this is the case, I just have them stare straight ahead and ask them not to look around. I usually have a candle they can gaze upon.

You will find most students keep their eyes closed, and the ones that want them open, eventually close them. The Classic Usui Reiki Attunement is taught with the student's eyes closed. This might offend some Reiki Masters because I allow the student to decide what they are comfortable with. It really does not matter, the Reiki Attunements are passed either way.

I also give the student(s) an overview of what to expect during the attunement, what I will be doing (placing symbols in Chakras) and what to expect after the attunement. With some of my Reiki Attunements I was never given an explanation for the attunements and I was unhappy with that. I was just given the instructions, then put in a dark room and told to keep my eyes closed. I did receive the attunements, but I always had unanswered questions. I recommend keeping the student fully informed of the whole process. I have found students have liked this philosophy and it has made a difference with their understanding of Reiki and its use.

Instructions for Students

The following photos are the instructions I give and have the student(s) practice before the attunement. They sit on a stool or straight back chair so I can maneuver easily to the front and back.

1. The student starts with the hands in a prayer position in front of Heart Chakra.

2. The student raises their hands over the head when the Reiki Master touches the shoulder.

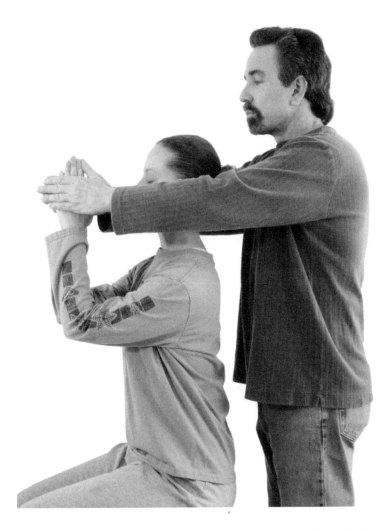

3. Hands are lowered back into prayer position in front of Heart Chakra.

4. Hands open palms up.

5. Hands closed and back into prayer position.

The student will sometimes fail to raise his or her hands when the shoulder is touched, if that happens, I just gently raise them.

I then give the student(s) an overview of the Reiki Attunement and what to expect during and after. If a student would like to keep his or her eyes open, that is OK, but they must look straight ahead.

How to give the various Reiki Attunements are explained in the following chapters.

Preparation

The following is a list I was given by one of my Reiki Teachers to use before giving or receiving a Reiki Attunement. I personally only do some of the preparations. What I recommend is to read the list, and see what intuitively feels right for you. You can follow as many suggestions on the list as you like. Of course your Reiki Attunement will still be passed or received if you cannot do every suggestion on the list. The bottom line again is what works and feels comfortable for you. There are many great doctors that have a steak dinner before they operate, and there are just as many doctors that do not eat before surgery. Both groups have success in surgery.

1. Stop eating all animal protein three days before the attunement.

2. Consume only water or juice for one to three days before the attunement. I recommend only a fast of four

to six hours before the attunement, unless you have had previous experiences with fasts.

3. Limit or stop your use of caffeine drinks one to three days before the attunement.

4. Stop drinking alcohol three days before the attunement. And of course none on the day of the attunement.

5. Limit sugar one to three days before the attunement.

6. Limit or stop smoking one to three days before the attunement.

7. Meditate an hour a day for at least a week using a style you are familiar with or simply spend this time in silence.

8. Limit TV, radio, movies and any outside distractions one to three days before the attunement.

9. One week before the attunement, meditate daily upon the reasons you want to receive the attunement.

10. Clear and release as much anger, fear, jealousy, hate, and worry you can before the attunement.

How the Reiki Master Prepares for the Attunement

I recommend the Reiki Master clear the room before he or she gives a Reiki Attunement. The best way is to use the Master Symbol and Power Symbol on the corners and center of the room. Drawing the two Reiki Symbols and/or visualizing them in the air can do this. You can also include bringing white healing light and Reiki energy to the room and /or smudge the room with sage. I usually do all the above. Also, when I know I have Reiki Attunements to give, I will send Reiki ahead of time to the area where the attunements will take place. This way when I show up the Reiki will already be there to start cleansing, clearing and preparing the area. As an option, you can also sage (smudge) the student(s) and yourself before you give the instructions for the attunement.

Before any Reiki Master passes any attunements, he or she should ground and clear him or herself. When I say clear, this means releasing any and all blockages you might have at the time. This will ensure Reiki will flow through the Master strongly and uninterrupted. This can be done in several ways and every Reiki Master has their own method and /or preferences for doing this. What I do is put all four Reiki Symbols in the palm of my hands, then put my hands on all my Chakras in front for 30 seconds or so, moving from the bottom on up. While I am doing this I have the intent to be cleared and grounded. When I am done with this, I take a moment and bring Reiki Energy through the top of my head (Crown Chakra) all the way down into the earth, then I wait a few seconds, and bring it all the way back up and out my Crown Chakra. This whole process should only take a few minutes. You can do your own process, as long as it balances, clears and grounds you before the attunement.

There are several more things a Reiki Master should do before the attunements are performed. Right before the attunement starts and while standing behind the seated student(s), all four Reiki Symbols are drawn into the Heart Chakra of the Master, and then in the space in front of the Master. Then the Reiki Master states silently the intent (type) of the attunement to be performed. This can also be included in prayer before the attunement starts. Then the attunement can commence.

Master's Step-By-Step Instructions for an Attunement

◆ Reiki Master prepares the room where the attunements are to be given.

◆ Reiki Master clears and grounds him or herself.

◆ Reiki Master gives instructions and explains process to the student(s).

◆ Student(s) sitting down with hands in prayer position ready for the attunement.

◆ Reiki Master is standing behind student(s), places all four Reiki Symbols in Heart Chakra and space in front of him or herself. States silently attunement intentions which can be included in a prayer.

◆ Attunement begins.

"Three things cannot be long hidden: the sun, the moon, and the truth."

-Buddha

Chapter Five

1st Level Reiki Attunement

In the following chapters in the Reiki Attunement instructions I use my right hand, but, if you are left handed, you can switch the hand around without a problem.

If you discover variations in the attunement process from what you have been taught, do not worry. The same reasons for the variations of the Reiki Symbols apply to the Reiki Attunements. Continue giving the Reiki Attunements as you were taught, they do work.

In the attunement directions I ask you to visualize. Some Reiki Masters have a challenge visualizing. If that is the case, perform the best you can and just imagine or know where the symbols are and where you want them to be. This method will work in passing the attunements. As mentioned before, your intent is the most important element when performing Reiki Attunements.

Reiki 1st Level Attunement

The Usui Reiki 1st Level Attunement consists of four separate attunements. These four attunements can be done in one day, or over several days. I myself, as with many Reiki Masters incorporate all four 1st Level Attunements into one. I will also show you how to do this at the end of the chapter. It depends on your circumstances and your preferences in what option you use in giving Reiki 1st Level Attunements. Both ways will pass the attunement successfully.

1st Level Attunement

During the 1st Level Reiki Attunement only the Power Symbol will be placed into the hands when they are in a prayer position above the head. Only the Power Symbol will be placed into the palms when they are opened face up in front of the Heart Chakra. This is done in all four attunements.

What happens after a 1st Level Attunement

◆ You are now a Reiki Healer.

◆ Your Chakras are opened and you are connected to the Reiki source.

◆ You are able to channel Reiki through your Palm Chakras to yourself and others by your link to the Reiki Source.

◆ Your experience with time and space will be different.

◆ You will become increasingly aware of what you need to do in regards to your healing.

◆ You will become more intuitive and psychic.

◆ Further changes will manifest in your life that are needed and distinctive for you.

The following are the instructions for the 1st Level Reiki Attunement

First Attunement for 1st Level

1st Part from the back

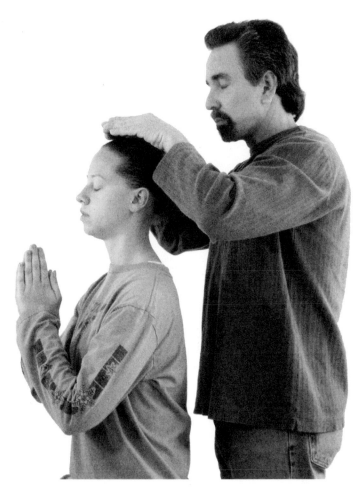

1. I place both hands on top of the head of the student meditating for 15 to 30 seconds to start the Reiki connection with the student.

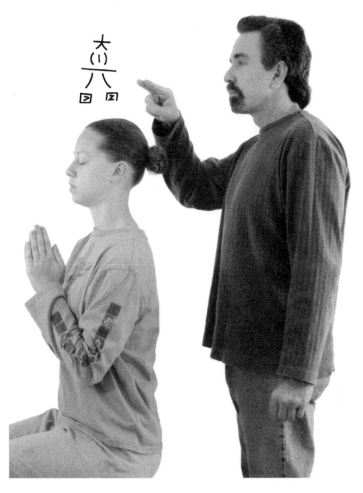

2. The Master Symbol is drawn over the head while I silently state the name of the symbol three times. Next I visualize the symbol drawn in the air moving into the Crown Chakra through the head and stopping at the base of the brain. Some Reiki Masters will also guide the symbol to the base of the brain with their right hand.

97

3. The student's left shoulder is touched indicating it is time to raise the hands still in a prayer position over their head (Crown Chakra).

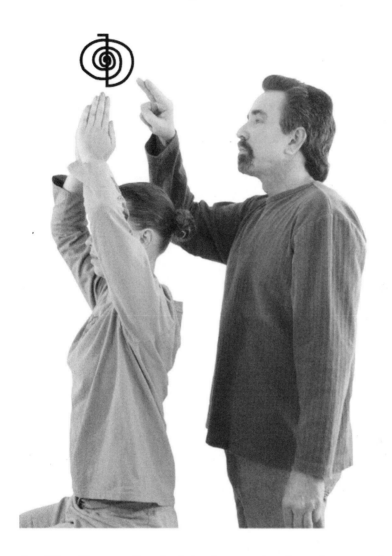

4. The Power Symbol is drawn in the air over the hands in prayer. The symbol is visualized going down the hands, into the Crown Chakra and stopping at the base of the brain. While this is being done, I state the symbol's name silently three times. This symbol can also be guided by the right hand.

5. Finally, I guide the hands still in a prayer position back in front of the Heart Chakra.

2nd Part from the front

1. I move to the front of the student and open the hands palms up and flat with my right hand. The palms are then held from underneath with my left hand.

2. The Power Symbol is drawn in the air in front of the student's third eye with the available right hand. The name of the symbol is stated silently three times as I visualize it going straight into the third eye.

3. I then draw the Power Symbol in the air over the palms held opened by my left hand. The name of the symbol is said silently three times as I visualize it going straight into the palms of the hands. I gently slap the palms three times.

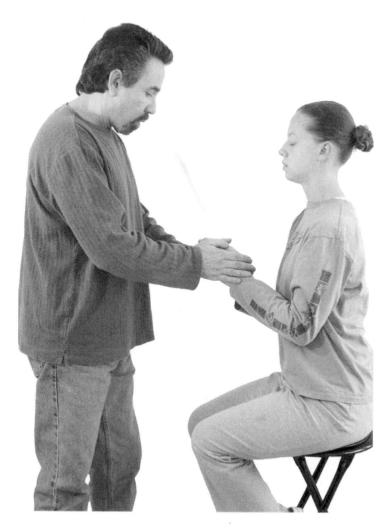

4. The hands are guided together into the prayer position and back to the front of the Heart Chakra. I then blow over the hands in a prayer position, and keep blowing up to the third eye and Crown Chakra, then down to the naval and back up to the hands.

3rd Part from the back

1. I place my hands on the student's shoulder and look down the Crown Chakra visualizing into the Heart Chakra. I place an affirmation into the heart and say it silently three times. A Reiki Master can have their own personal affirmation. The affirmation I use is, "Now this student is a powerful and aware Reiki Healer."

2. I bring my hands to the base of the student's head with the thumbs placed at the base of the skull. Then I state, "I now seal this process with Divine love and wisdom," silently while visualizing a door opening on the back of the head and the Power Symbol going in, then the door being closed and sealed. The student has now connected directly to the Reiki source.

3. I put my hands on the student's shoulder and give a blessing which is, "We are both blessed by this process."

4. I move to the front, and ask the student to place his or her palms on their legs and to breathe deeply and slowly while opening their eyes. *This is the completion of the first attunement for the 1st Level.*

Second Attunement for 1st Level

1st Part from the back

1. I place both hands on top of the head of the student meditating for 15 to 30 seconds to start the Reiki connection with the student.

2. The Master Symbol is drawn over the head while I silently state the name of the symbol three times. I visualize the symbol drawn in the air moving into the Crown Chakra through the head and stopping at the base of the brain. Some Reiki Masters will also guide the symbol to the base of the brain with their right hand.

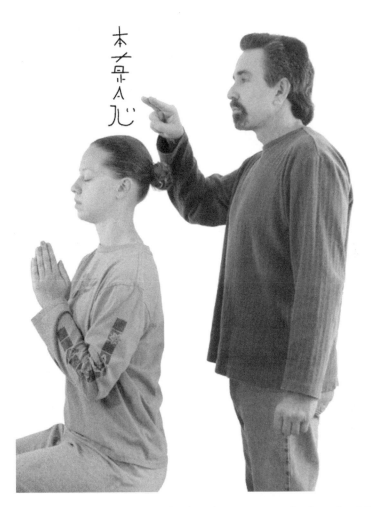

3. The Long Distance Symbol is drawn over the head while I silently state the name of the symbol three times. I then visualize the Symbol drawn in the air moving into the Crown Chakra through the head and stopping at the base of the brain. Some Reiki Masters will also guide the symbol to the base of the brain with their right hand.

4. Then the student's left shoulder is touched indicating it is time to raise the hands still in a prayer position over their head (Crown Chakra).

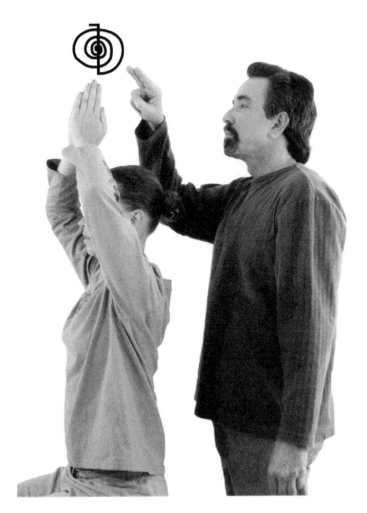

5. Next the Power Symbol is drawn in the air over the hands in prayer. The symbol is then visualized going down the hands, into the Crown Chakra and stopping at the base of the brain. While this is being done, I state the symbol's name silently three times. This symbol can also be guided by the right hand.

6. I then guide the hands still in a prayer position back in front of the Heart Chakra.

2nd Part from the front

1. I move to the front of the student and open the hands palms up and flat with my right hand. The palms are then held from underneath with my left hand.

2. The Power Symbol is drawn in the air in front of the student's third eye with the available right hand. The name of the symbol is stated silently three times as I visualize it going straight into the third eye.

3. The Long Distance Symbol is drawn in the air in front of the student's third eye with the available right hand. The name of the symbol is stated silently three times as I visualize it going straight into the third eye.

4. I then draw the Power Symbol in the air over the palms held opened by my left hand. The name of the symbol is said silently three times as I visualize it going straight into the palms of the hands. I gently slap the palms three times.

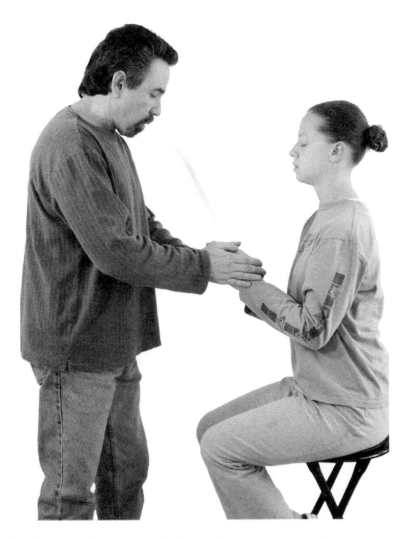

5. The hands are guided back together to the prayer position and back to the front of the Heart Chakra. I blow over the hands in a prayer position, and keep blowing up to the third eye and Crown Chakra, then down to the naval and back up to the hands.

3rd Part from the back

1. I place my hands on the student's shoulders and look down the Crown Chakra visualizing into the Heart Chakra. I place an affirmation into the heart and say it silently three times. A Reiki Master can have their own personal affirmation. The affirmation I use is, "Now this student is a powerful and aware Reiki Healer."

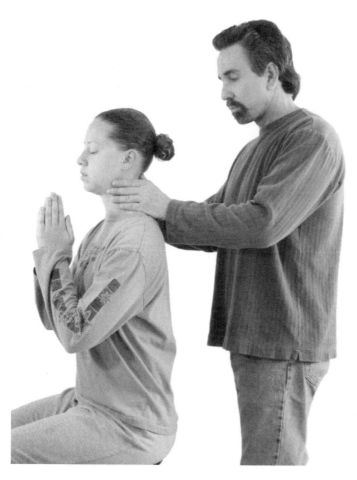

2. I bring my hands to the base of the student's head with the thumbs placed at the base of the skull. Then I state, "I now seal this process with Divine love and wisdom" silently while visualizing a door opening on the back of the head and the Power Symbol going in, then the door being closed and sealed. The student has now connected directly to the Reiki source.

3. I put my hands on the student's shoulders and give a blessing which is, "We are both blessed by this process."

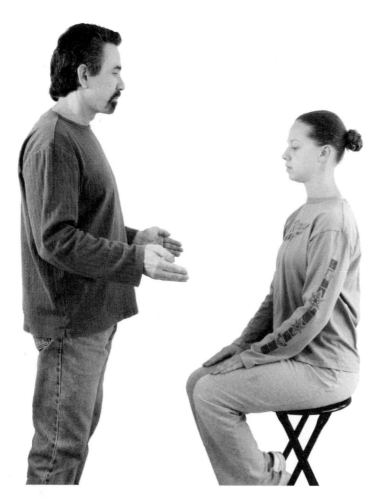

4. I move to the front, and then ask the student to place his or her palms on their legs and to breathe deeply and slowly while opening their eyes. *This is the completion of the second attunement for the 1st Level.*

Third Attunement for 1ˢᵗ Level

The 3ʳᵈ attunement is identical to the 2ⁿᵈ attunement. For the 3ʳᵈ attunement, the 2ⁿᵈ attunement is repeated.

Fourth Attunement for 1st Level

1st Part from the back

1. I place both hands on top of the head of the student meditating for 15 to 30 seconds to start the Reiki connection with the student.

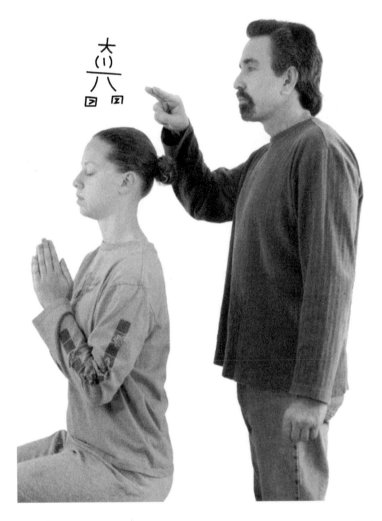

2. The Master Symbol is drawn over the head while I silently state the name of the symbol three times. I visualize the symbol drawn in the air moving into the Crown Chakra through the head and ending up at the base of the brain. Some Reiki Masters will also guide the symbol to the base of the brain with their right hand.

126

3. The Long Distance Symbol is drawn over the head while I silently state the name of the symbol three times. I then visualize the symbol drawn in the air moving into the Crown Chakra through the head and ending up at the base of the brain. Some Reiki Masters will also guide the symbol to the base of the brain with their right hand.

127

4. The Mental/Emotional Symbol is drawn over the head while I silently state the name of the symbol three times. I visualize the symbol drawn in the air moving into the Crown Chakra through the head and ending up at the base of the brain. Some Reiki Masters will also guide the symbol to the base of the brain with their right hand.

5. The student's left shoulder is then touched indicating it is time to raise the hands still in a prayer position over their head (Crown Chakra).

6. The Power Symbol is drawn in the air over the hands in prayer. The symbol is then visualized going down the hands, into the Crown Chakra and stopping at the base of the brain. While this is being done, I state the symbol's name silently three times. This symbol can also be guided by the right hand.

7. I then guide the hands still in a prayer position back in front of the Heart Chakra.

2ⁿᵈ Part from the front

1. I move to the front of the student and open the hands palms up and flat with my right hand. The palms are then held from underneath with my left hand.

2. The Power Symbol is drawn in the air in front of the student's third eye with the available right hand. The name of the symbol is stated silently three times as I visualize it going straight into the third eye.

3. The Long Distance Symbol is drawn in the air in front of the student's third eye with the available right hand. The name of the symbol is stated silently three times as I visualize it going straight into the third eye.

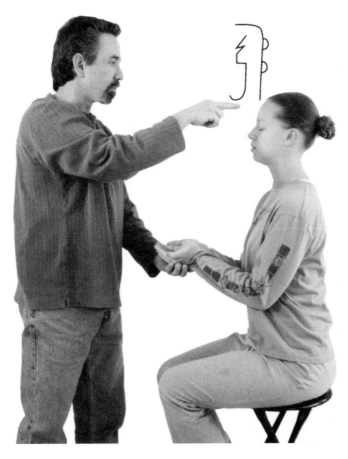

4. The Mental/Emotional Symbol is drawn in the air in front of the student's third eye with the available right hand. The name of the symbol is stated silently three times as I visualize it going straight into the third eye.

5. I then draw the Power Symbol in the air over the palms held opened by my left hand. The name of the symbol is said silently three times as I visualize it going straight into the palms of the hands. I gently slap the palms three times.

6. The hands are guided back together to the prayer position and back to the front of the Heart Chakra. I then blow over the hands in a prayer position, and keep blowing up to the third eye and Crown Chakra, then down to the naval and back up to the hands.

3rd Part from the back

1. I place my hands on the student's shoulders and look down the Crown Chakra visualizing into the Heart Chakra. I then place an affirmation into the heart and say it silently three times. A Reiki Master can have their own personal affirmation. The affirmation I use is, "Now this student is a powerful and aware Reiki Healer."

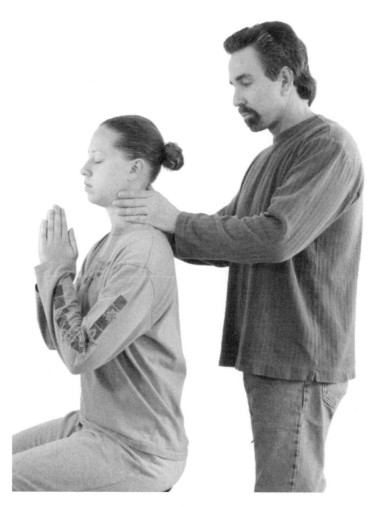

2. I bring my hands to the base of the student's head with the thumbs placed at the base of the skull. Then I state, "I now seal this process with Divine love and wisdom" silently while visualizing a door opening on the back of the head and the Power Symbol going in, then the door being closed and sealed. The student has now connected directly to the Reiki source.

3. I put my hands on the student's shoulders and give a blessing which is, "We are both blessed by this process."

4. I move to the front, and ask the student to place his or her palms on their legs and to breathe deeply and slowly while opening their eyes. *After this fourth Attunement, the Reiki 1st Level Attunement is complete.*

The following are the instructions for the Reiki 1ˢᵗ Level Attunement in only one attunement. This can be used as an option instead of the 1ˢᵗ Level Attunement with the four separate attunements. This is the attunement I use. Both ways will pass the attunement.

You prepare for the attunement in the same way. But, when you state your intent on what type of attunement you are going to give, add that you are going to include all four 1ˢᵗ level Reiki attunements into one.

Reiki 1st Level Attunement In One Attunement

1st Part from the back

1. I place both hands on top of the head of the student meditating for 15 to 30 seconds to start the Reiki connection with the student.

2. The Master Symbol is drawn over the head while I silently state the name of the symbol six times. I visualize the symbol drawn in the air moving into the Crown Chakra through the head and then stopping at the base of the brain. Some Reiki Masters will also guide the symbol to the base of the brain with their right hand.

3. The student's left shoulder is then touched indicating it is time to raise the hands, still in a prayer position over their head (Crown Chakra).

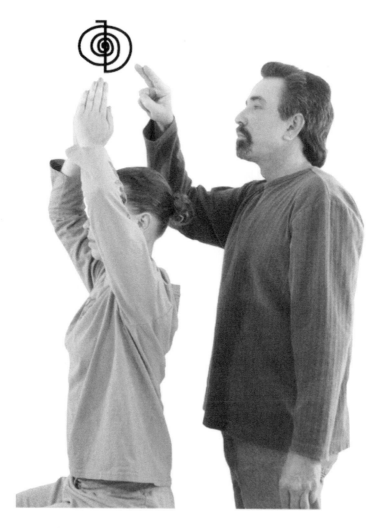

4. The Power Symbol is drawn in the air over the hands in prayer. The symbol is then visualized going down the hands, into the Crown Chakra and stopping at the base of the brain. While this is being done, I state the symbol's name silently six times. This symbol can also be guided by the right hand.

146

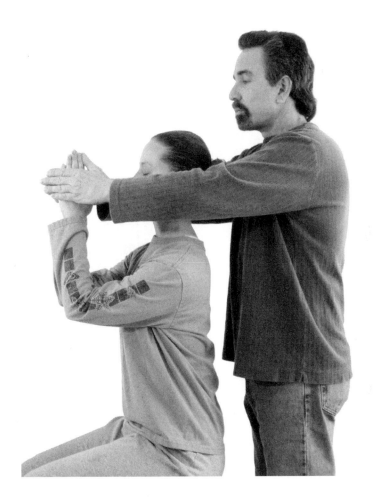

5. I then guide the hands still in a prayer position back in front of the Heart Chakra.

6. The Long Distance Symbol is drawn over the head while I silently state the name of the symbol six times. I then visualize the symbol drawn in the air moving into the Crown Chakra through the head and stopping and ending up at the base of the brain. Some Reiki Masters will also guide the symbol to the base of the brain with their right hand.

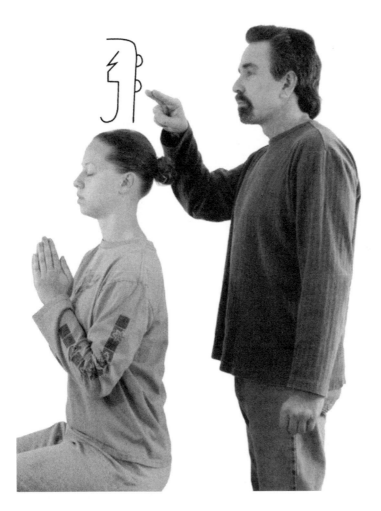

7. The Mental/Emotional Symbol is drawn over the head while I silently state the name of the symbol six times. I then visualize the symbol drawn in the air moving into the Crown Chakra through the head and stopping and ending up at the base of the brain. Some Reiki Masters will also guide the symbol to the base of the brain with their right hand.

8. The student's left shoulder is then touched indicating it is time to raise the hands, still in a prayer position over their head (Crown Chakra).

9. The Power Symbol is then drawn in the air over the hands in prayer. The symbol is visualized going down the hands, into the Crown Chakra and stopping at the base of the brain. While this is being done, I state the symbol's name silently six times. This symbol can also be guided by the right hand.

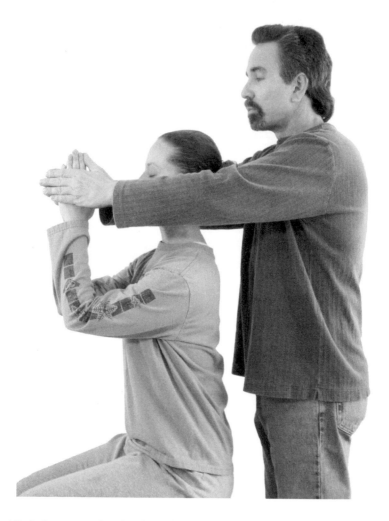

10. I then guide the hands still in a prayer position back in front of the Heart Chakra.

2nd Part from the front

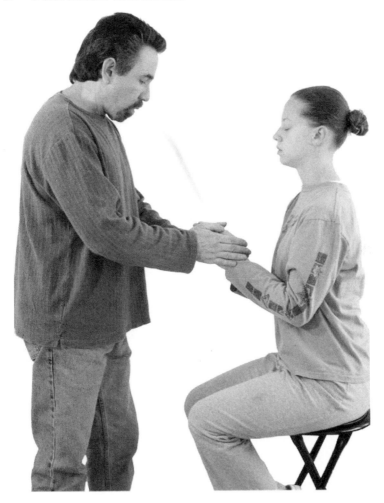

1. I move to the front of the student and open the hands palms up and flat with my right hand. The palms are then held from underneath with my left hand.

2. The Power Symbol is drawn in the air in front of the student's third eye with the available right hand. The name of the symbol is stated silently six times as I visualize it going straight into the third eye.

3. I then draw the Power Symbol in the air over the palms held open by my left hand. The name of the symbol is said silently six times as I visualize it going straight into the palms of the hands. I gently slap the palms six times.

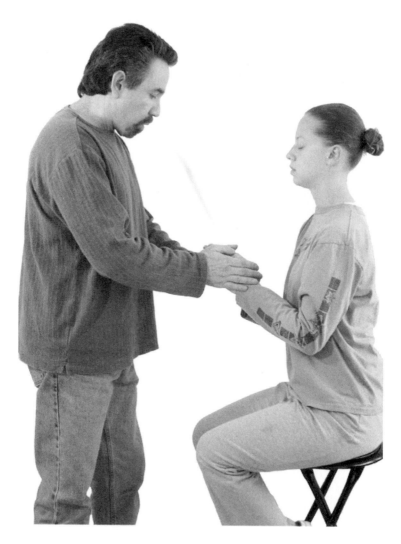

4. The student's hands are guided into to the prayer position and back to the front of the Heart Chakra. I then blow over the hands in a prayer position, and keep blowing up to the third eye and Crown Chakra, then down to the naval and back up to the hands.

5. The Long Distance Symbol is drawn in the air in front of the third eye with the available right hand. The name of the symbol is stated silently six times as I visualize it going straight into the third eye.

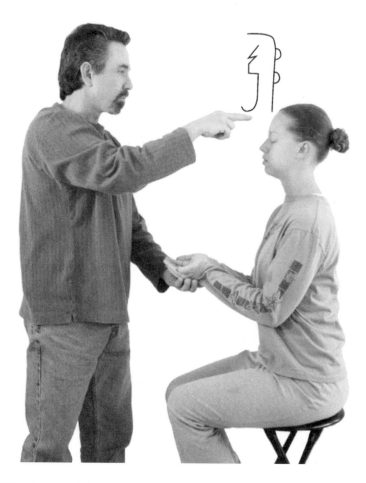

6. The Mental/Emotional Symbol is drawn in the air in front of the third eye with the available right hand. The name of the symbol is stated silently six times as I visualize it going straight into the third eye.

7. I then draw the Power Symbol in the air over the palms held opened by my left hand. The name of the symbol is said silently six times as I visualize it going straight into the palms of the hands. I gently slap the palms six times.

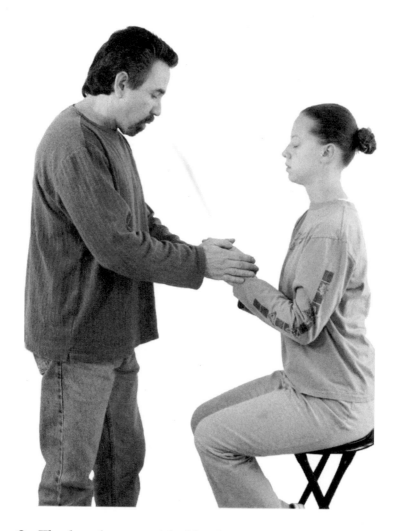

8. The hands are guided back together into the prayer position and back to the front of the Heart Chakra. I then blow over the hands in a prayer position, and keep blowing up to the third eye and Crown Chakra, then down to the naval and back up to the hands.

3rd Part from the back

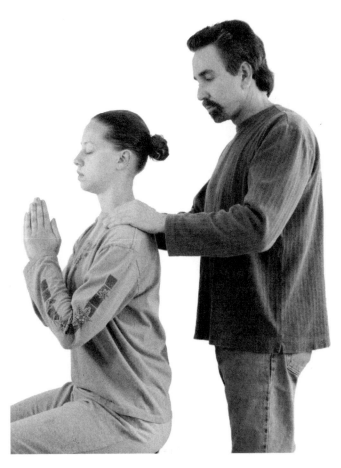

1. I place my hands on the student's shoulders and look down the Crown Chakra visualizing into the Heart Chakra. I then place an affirmation into the heart and say it silently six times. A Reiki Master can have their own personal affirmation. The affirmation I use is, "Now this student is a powerful and aware Reiki Healer."

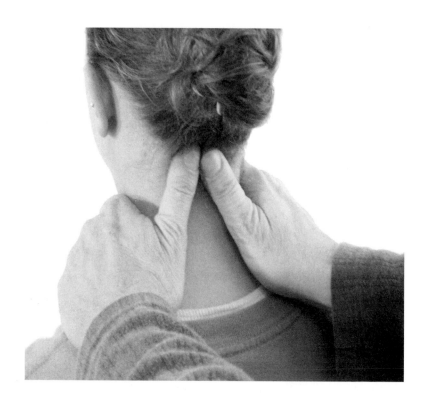

2. I bring my hands to the base of the head with the thumbs placed at the base of the skull. Then I state, "I now seal this process with Divine love and wisdom" silently while visualizing a door opening on the back of the head and the Power Symbol going in, then the door being closed and sealed. The student has now connected directly to the Reiki source.

3. I put my hands on the student's shoulder and give a blessing which is, "We are both blessed by this process."

4. I move to the front, and then ask the student to place his or her palms on their legs and to breathe deeply and slowly while opening their eyes. *The Reiki 1st Level Attunement is complete.*

"Work out your own salvation. Do not depend on others."

-Buddha

"Just as a candle cannot burn without fire, man cannot live without a spiritual life."

-Buddha

Chapter Six

2nd Level Reiki Attunement

In the Reiki 2nd Level Attunement the Power, Mental/Emotional and the Long Distance Symbols are placed into the hands while they are in a prayer position over the head. They are also placed into the palms when they are opened face up in front of the Heart Chakra. Placing the symbols in these areas enables the student to activate these three symbols. There is only one attunement for the 2nd Level.

What happens after a 2nd Level Attunement:

♦ When you are a 2nd Level Healer you are able to manifest what you need in your life at a faster pace.

♦ Your Reiki healing energy will flow at a stronger and higher vibration.

♦ Your Reiki awareness will continue to expand with your experience and progress.

♦ You will have three powerful Reiki Symbols to use and activate.

♦ You will be able to activate the symbols by themselves, or combine them for different healing situations.

♦ Your Reiki sessions can be reduced to less time.

♦ Restrictions of time and space will no longer exist. You can now send Reiki to the past, present and future.

♦ You will become more aware of the intensity, flow and the power of Reiki.

♦ You will become more intuitive and psychic.

♦ Further changes will manifest in your life that are needed and unique for you.

The following are the instructions for the Reiki 2nd Level Attunement

Reiki 2nd Level Attunement

1st Part from the back

1. I place both hands on top of the head of the student meditating for 15 to 30 seconds to start the Reiki connection with the student.

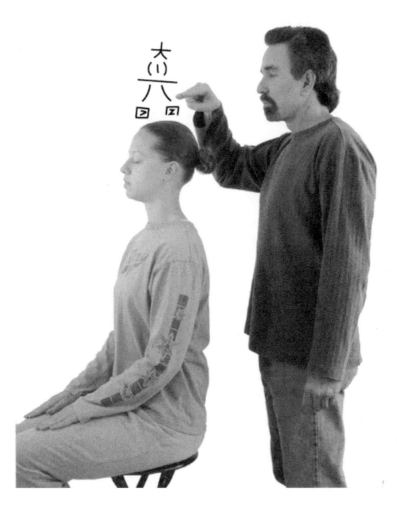

2. The Master Symbol is drawn over the head while I silently state the name of the symbol three times. I then visualize the symbol drawn in the air moving into the Crown Chakra through the head and then stopping at the base of the brain. Some Reiki Masters will also guide the symbol to the base of the brain with their right hand.

3. The student's left shoulder is then touched indicating it is time to raise the hands, still in a prayer position over their head (Crown Chakra).

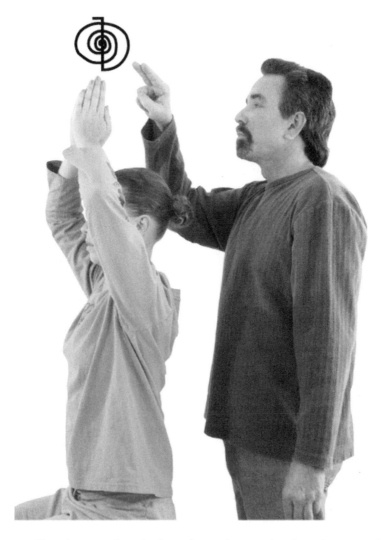

4. The Power Symbol is then drawn in the air over the hands in prayer. The symbol is visualized going down the hands, into the Crown Chakra and stopping at the base of the brain. While this is being done, I state the symbol's name silently three times. This symbol can also be guided by the right hand.

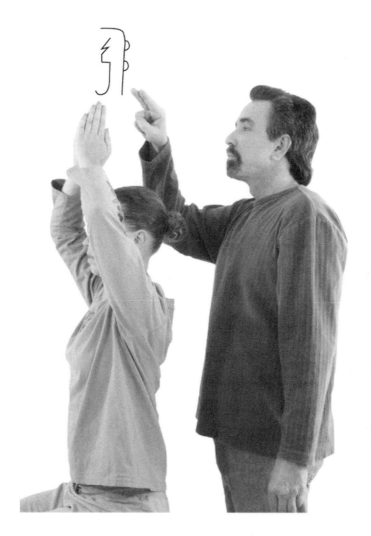

5. The Mental/ Emotional Symbol is then drawn in the air over the hands in prayer. The symbol is visualized going down the hands, into the Crown Chakra and then stopping at the base of the brain. While this is being done, I state the symbol's name silently three times. This symbol can also be guided by the right hand.

173

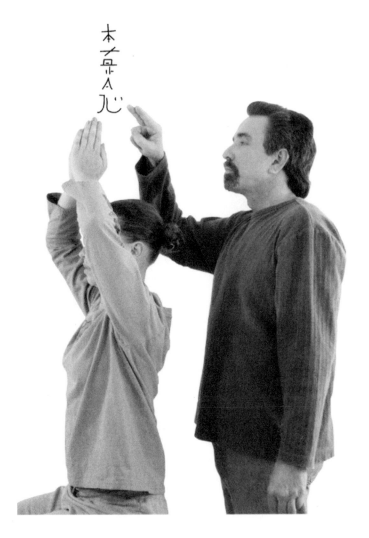

6. The Long Distance Symbol is then drawn in the air over the hands in prayer position. The symbol is visualized going down the hands, into the Crown Chakra and stopping at the base of the brain. While this is being done, I state the symbol's name silently three times. This symbol can also be guided by the right hand.

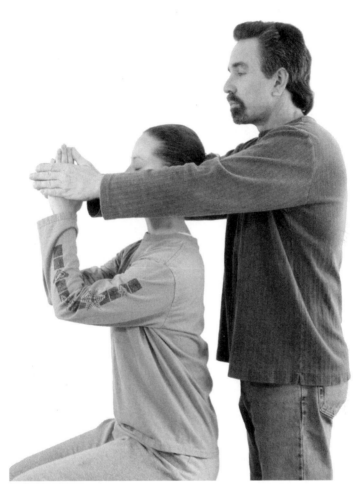

7. I then guide the hands, still in a prayer position back in front of the Heart Chakra.

2nd Part from the front

1. I move to the front of the student and open the hands palms up and flat with my right hand. The palms are then held from underneath with my left hand.

2. The Power Symbol is drawn in the air in front of the student's third eye with the available right hand. The name of the symbol is stated silently three times as I visualize it going straight into the third eye.

3. The Mental/Emotional Symbol is drawn in the air in front of the third eye with the available right hand. The name of the symbol is stated silently three times as I visualize it going straight into the third eye.

4. The Long Distance Symbol is drawn in the air in front of the third eye with the available right hand. The name of the symbol is stated silently three times as I visualize it going straight into the third eye.

5. I draw the Power Symbol in the air over the palms held opened by my left hand. The name of the symbol is said silently three times as I visualize it going straight into the palms of the hands. I gently slap the palms three times.

6. I draw the Mental/Emotional Symbol in the air over the palms held opened by my left hand. The name of the symbol is said silently three times as I visualize it going straight into the palms of the hands. I gently slap the palms three times.

7. I then draw the Long Distance Symbol in the air over the palms held opened by my left hand. The name of the symbol is said silently three times as I visualize it going straight into the palms of the hands. I gently slap the palms three times.

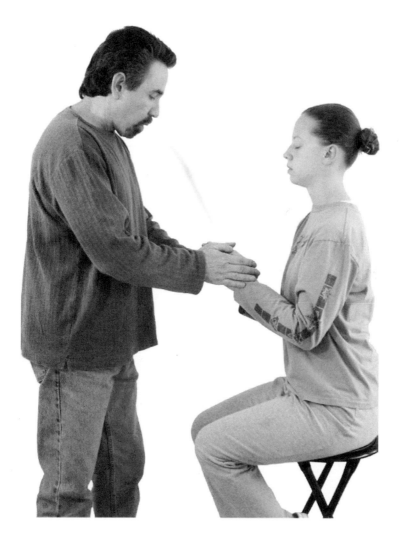

8. The hands are guided back together in the prayer position at the front of the Heart Chakra. I then blow over the hands in a prayer position, and keep blowing up to the third eye and Crown Chakra, then down to the naval and back up to the hands.

3ʳᵈ Part from the back

1. I place my hands on the student's shoulders and look down the Crown Chakra visualizing into the Heart Chakra. I then place an affirmation into the heart and say it silently three times. A Reiki Master can have their own personal affirmation. The affirmation I use is, "Now this student is a powerful and aware Reiki Healer."

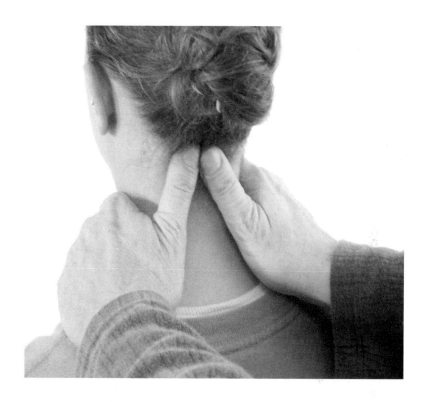

2. I bring my hands to the base of the student's head with the thumbs placed at the base of the skull. I state, "I now seal this process with Divine love and wisdom" silently while visualizing a door opening on the back of the head and the Power Symbol going in, then the door being closed and sealed. The student has now connected directly to the Reiki source.

3. I put my hands on the shoulders and give a blessing which is, "We are both blessed by this process."

4. I move to the front, and then ask the student to place his or her palms on their legs and to breathe deeply and slowly while opening their eyes. *The Reiki 2nd Level Attunement is complete.*

"Do not dwell in the past, do not dream of the future, concentrate the mind on the present moment."

-Buddha

Chapter Seven

Reiki Master Attunement

In the Reiki Master Level Attunements the Master, Power, Mental/Emotional and the Long Distance Symbols are placed into the hands while they are in a prayer position. They are also placed into the palms when they are opened face up in front of the Heart Chakra. This enables the student to activate the Master Symbol. There is only one attunement for the Master Level.

After receiving the Reiki Master Attunement you are able to give Reiki 1st, 2nd and Master Level as well as Psychic and Healing Attunements.

What happens after a Master Attunement

◆ Your healing energy will flow stronger and vibrate at a higher, more intense level. It will continue to expand at your own pace.

◆ Your personal and spiritual growth will expand to higher levels.

◆ You will have a Master Symbol that will intensify your other Reiki Symbols.

◆ You will become more at one with yourself and the universe.

◆ Your awareness of the intensity and the power of Reiki will expand.

◆ You will become more intuitive and psychic.

◆ The attunement and symbol will help you in your own life where they are needed.

◆ You will have a greater feeling of wholeness, fulfillment and completion.

◆ All the qualities of Reiki are enhanced by the use of the Master Symbol.

◆ Further changes will manifest in your life that are needed and unique for you.

The following are the Instructions for the Reiki Master Level Attunement.

Reiki Master Attunement.

1st Part from the back

1. I place both hands on top of the head of the student meditating for 15 to 30 seconds to start the Reiki connection with the student.

2. The student's left shoulder is then touched indicating it is time to raise the hands still in a prayer position over their head (Crown Chakra).

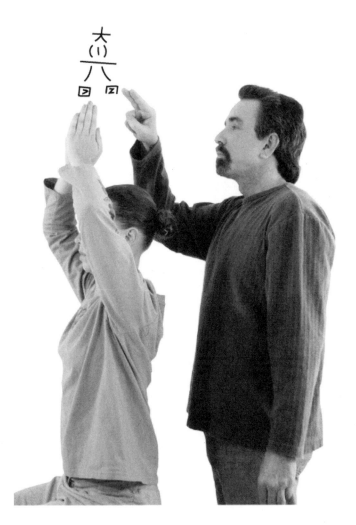

3. The Master Symbol is then drawn in the air over the hands in prayer position. Next the symbol is visualized going down the hands, into the Crown Chakra and stopping at the base of the brain. While this is being done, I state the symbol's name silently three times. This symbol can also be guided by the right hand.

4. The Power Symbol is then drawn in the air over the hands in prayer position. The symbol is visualized going down the hands, into the Crown Chakra and stopping at the base of the brain. While this is being done, I state the symbol's name silently three times. This symbol can also be guided by the right hand.

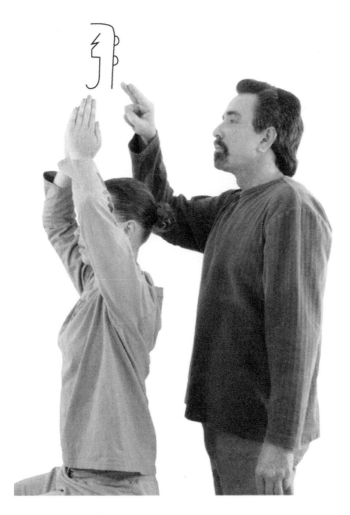

5. The Mental/Emotional Symbol is then drawn in the air over the hands in prayer position. The symbol is visualized going down the hands, into the Crown Chakra and stopping at the base of the brain. While this is being done, I state the symbol's name silently three times. This symbol can also be guided by the right hand.

195

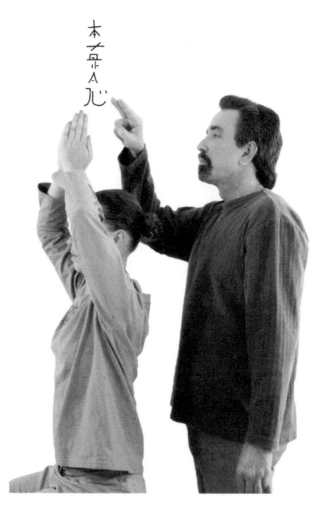

6. The Long Distance Symbol is drawn in the air over the hands in prayer position. The symbol is visualized going down the hands, into the Crown Chakra and stopping at the base of the brain. While this is being done, I state the symbol's name silently three times. This symbol can also be guided by the right hand.

7. I then guide the hands still in a prayer position back in front of the Heart Chakra.

2nd Part from the front

1. I move to the front of the student and open the hands palms up and flat with my right hand. The palms are held from underneath with my left hand.

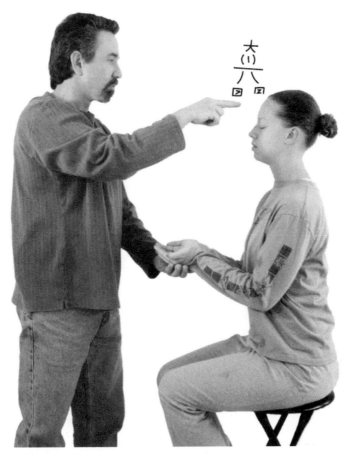

2. The Master Symbol is drawn in the air in front of the student's third eye with the available right hand. The name of the symbol is stated silently three times as I visualize it going straight into the third eye.

3. The Power Symbol is drawn in the air in front of the student's third eye with the available right hand. The name of the symbol is stated silently three times as I visualize it going straight into the third eye.

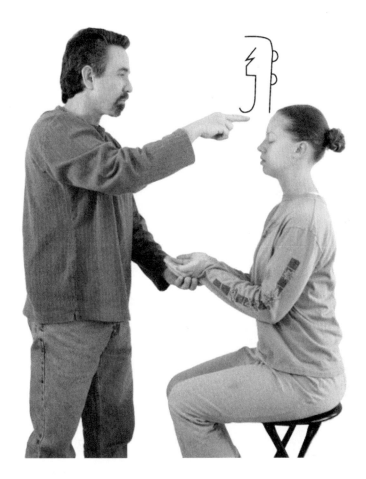

4. The Mental/Emotional Symbol is drawn in the air in front of the student's third eye with the available right hand. The name of the symbol is stated silently three times as I visualize it going straight into the third eye.

5. The Long Distance Symbol is drawn in the air in front of the third eye with the available right hand. The name of the symbol is stated silently three times as I visualize it going straight into the third eye.

6. I draw the Master Symbol in the air over the palms held opened by my left hand. The name of the symbol is said silently three times as I visualize it going straight into the palms of the hands. I gently slap the palms three times.

7. I draw the Power Symbol in the air over the palms held opened by my left hand. The name of the symbol is said silently three times as I visualize it going straight into the palms of the hands. I gently slap the palms three times.

8. I draw the Mental/Emotional Symbol in the air over the palms held opened by my left hand. The name of the symbol is said silently three times as I visualize it going straight into the palms of the hands. I gently slap the palms three times.

9. I then draw the Long Distance Symbol in the air over the palms held opened by my left hand. The name of the symbol is said silently three times as I visualize it going straight into the palms of the hands. I gently slap the palms three times.

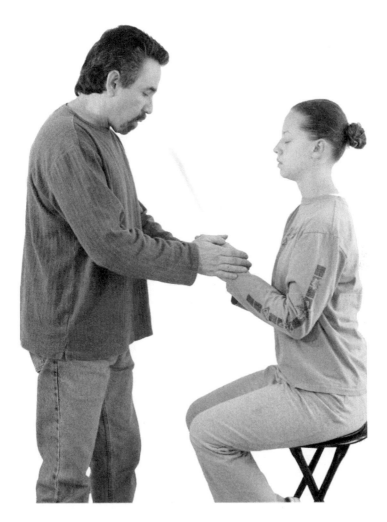

10. The hands are guided back to the prayer position and back to the front of the Heart Chakra. I then blow over the hands in a prayer position, and keep blowing up to the third eye and Crown Chakra, then down to the naval and back up to the hands.

3rd Part from the back

1. I place my hands on the student's shoulders and look down the Crown Chakra visualizing into the Heart Chakra. I then place an affirmation into the heart and say it silently three times. A Reiki Master can have their own personal affirmation. The affirmation I use is, "Now this student is a powerful and aware Reiki Healer."

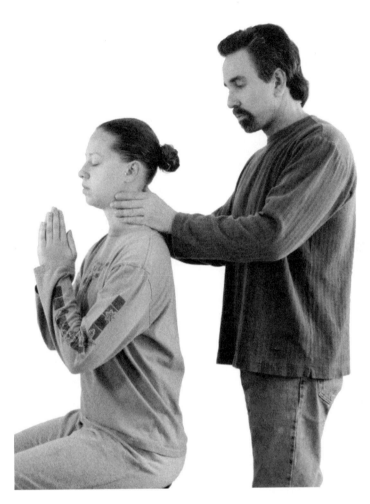

2. I bring my hands to the base of the head with the thumbs placed at the base of the skull. Then I state, "I now seal this process with Divine love and wisdom" silently while visualizing a door opening on the back of the head and the Power Symbol going in, then the door being closed and sealed. The student has now connected directly to the Reiki source.

3. I put my hands on the student's shoulders and give a blessing which is, "We are both blessed by this process."

4. I move to the front, and then ask the student to place his or her palms on their legs and to breathe deeply and slowly while opening their eyes. *The Reiki Master Level Attunement is complete.*

"We are what we think. All that we are arises with our thoughts. With our thoughts, we make the world."

-Buddha

Chapter Eight

Reiki Psychic Attunement

My Psychic Attunement program on video and DVD has helped many thousands of people open up their natural psychic abilities. Today it still remains one of the most popular attunement programs. This chapter gives you directions on how to perform this attunement. All the Reiki Attunements will help with psychic abilities, but this attunement works specifically on your psychic abilities. There is only one caveat with this attunement. Only receive it or give it to a student once every three to four weeks. On occasion a person will take the attunement over and over and they will start receiving too much information at once and be unable to process and/or understand it. They will become unbalanced and confused. There is no great harm because once they stop taking the attunement everything will catch and they will become balanced again. So take the attunement sparingly and wait and see what unfolds. You can receive all other Reiki Attunements as many times as you like for reinforcement.

What the Psychic Attunement Can Do

Being psychic is basically being aware of what's going on in your life. This includes people, places, things, events and yourself. It is being aware on all levels, mentally, physically, spiritually and emotionally. The Reiki Psychic Attunement helps with all of the above and will help open and expand your natural psychic abilities. It also helps clear your mental, spiritual, physical and emotional bodies so your psychic gifts can surface and/or expand.

The attunement doesn't give instant psychic powers, but opens up the person's natural psychic abilities. Everybody has a psychic gift or a combination of gifts. And of course not everybody explores them or expands them. For example if a person is clairvoyant, they will receive stronger, clearer messages with the attunement. A person that receives information in dreams, will experience more informative, clearer dreams. Usually the Psychic Attunement does not open a psychic ability a person is not aware of, but it does happen. This attunement at times has revealed new psychic abilities the person was not previously aware of.

The Psychic Attunement is a powerful tool and it will increase the psychic abilities of a person from wherever they are. Just because you consciously are unaware of any increase (shift) of psychic abilities after you receive the attunement, does not mean one is not happening. Most of the time it's a gradual, subtle shift with an accumulative effect on your psychic abilities. Your expanded awareness from the attunement might be as straightforward as making a good decision in your life or as far reaching as seeing future events.

Psychic Attunement

There are three parts to the attunement. With the Psychic Attunement you will be working with the Crown Chakra and Sixth Chakra (third eye). The person receiving the attunement just rests his or her hands in their lap. You prepare the same way for this attunement as with the other attunements, except your intent is to give a Psychic Attunement.

The following are the instructions for the Reiki Psychic Attunement. During the Attunement, when I visualize symbols stopping in the middle of the head, this area is straight across from the Sixth Chakra (third eye). The person keeps their hands in their lap.

Reiki Psychic Attunement

1st Part from the back

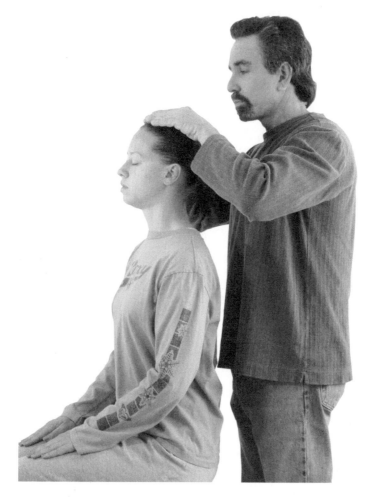

1. I place both hands on top of the head, meditating for 15 to 30 seconds to start the Reiki connection with the person.

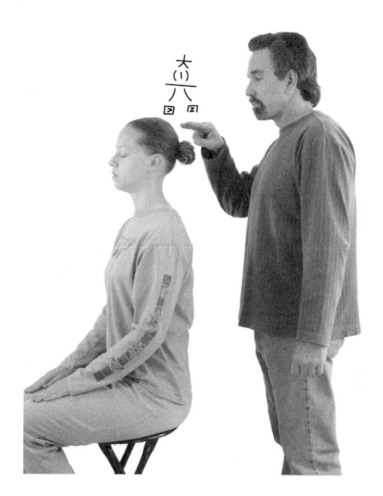

2. I draw the Master Symbol in the air at the back of the head and I visualize it going into the back of the head stopping in the middle. While this is being done, the symbol's name is said silently one time.

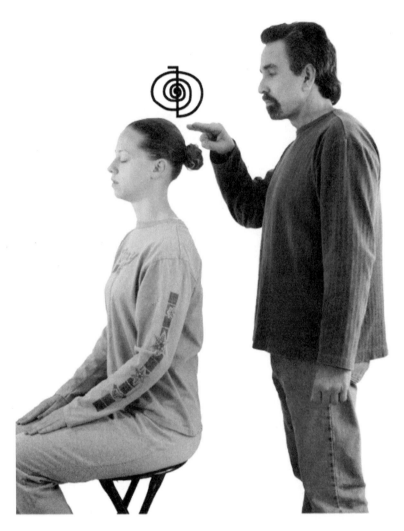

3. I draw the Power Symbol in the air at the back of the head and I visualize it going into the back of the head, stopping in the middle. While this is being done, the symbol's name is said silently one time.

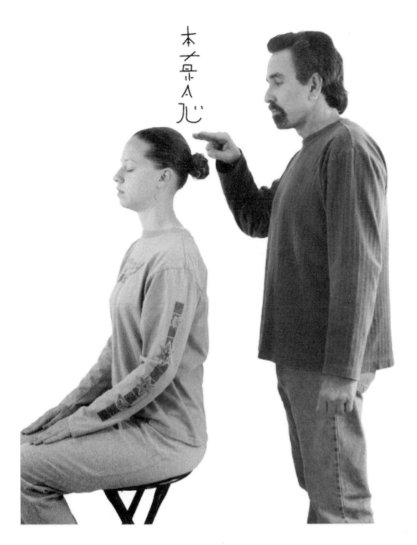

4. I draw the Long Distance Symbol in the air at the back of the head and I visualize it going into the back of the head, stopping in the middle. While this is being done, the symbol's name is said silently one time.

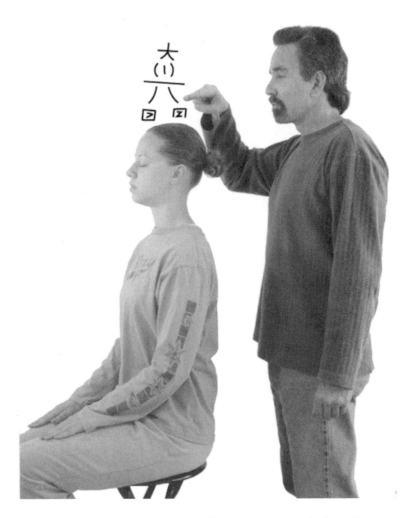

5. I draw the Master Symbol on top of the Crown Chakra and visualize it going into the top of the head, stopping in the middle. While this is being done, the symbol's name is said silently one time.

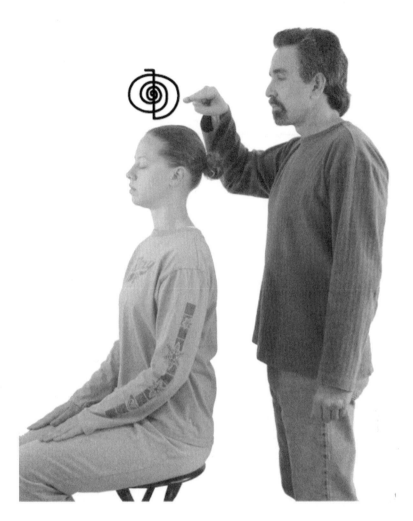

6. I draw the Power Symbol on top of the Crown Chakra and visualize it going into the top of the head, stopping in the middle. While this is being done, the symbol's name is said silently one time.

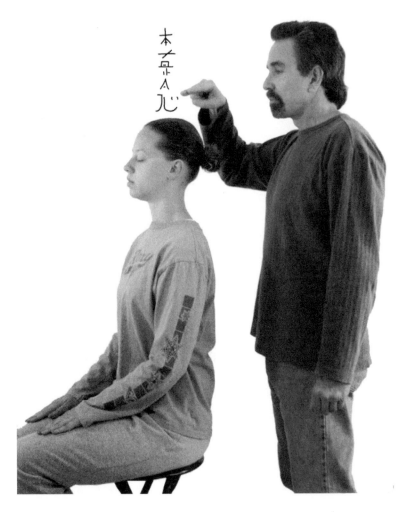

7. I draw the Long Distance Symbol on top of the Crown Chakra and visualize it going into the top of the head stopping in the middle. While this is being done, the symbol's name is said silently one time.

2nd Part from the front

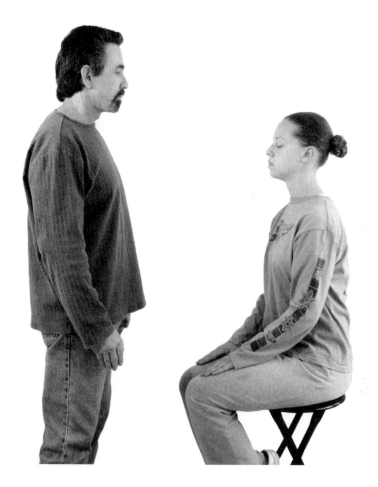

1. I step to the front of the person.

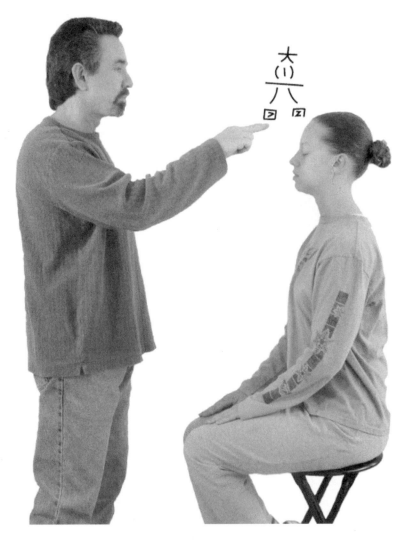

2. I draw the Master Symbol in front of the Sixth Chakra in the air and visualize it going into the third eye, stopping in the middle of the head. While this is being done, the symbol's name is said silently one time.

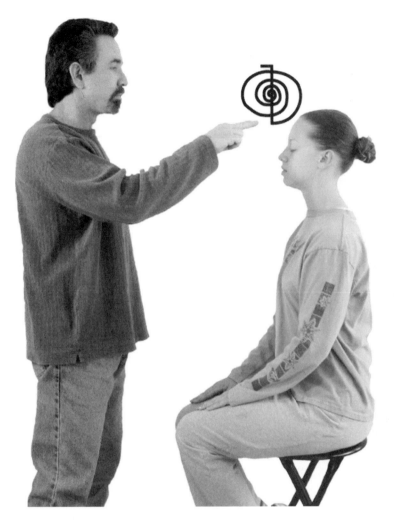

3. I draw the Power Symbol in front of the Sixth Chakra in the air and visualize it going into the third eye, stopping in the middle of the head. While this is being done, the symbol's name is said silently one time.

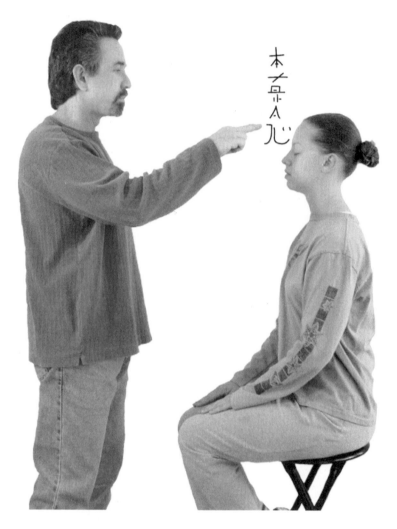

4. I draw the Long Distance Symbol in front of the Sixth Chakra in the air and visualize it going into the third eye, stopping in the middle of the head. While this is being done, the symbol's name is said silently one time.

5. Then, I lightly blow on the Sixth Chakra for a few seconds, and at the same time hold the intent that I am clearing and releasing any blockages in the Sixth Chakra.

3rd Part from the back

1. I go to the back of the person

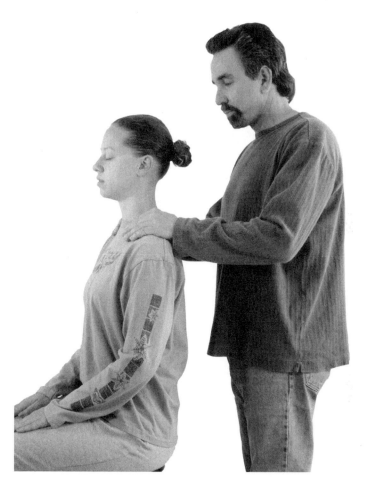

2. I place my hands on the shoulders and look down into the Crown Chakra, visualizing into the middle of the head, stopping where the Sixth Chakra comes straight across. I place a silent affirmation into that area three times. The affirmation is, " This person's psychic abilities are now fully opened."

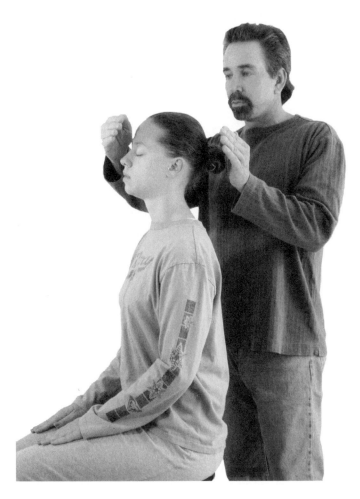

3. I then place one hand on the Sixth Chakra, and the other on the back of the head. I state silently, "I now seal this process with Divine love and wisdom" I keep my hands in that position for several minutes and channel Reiki.

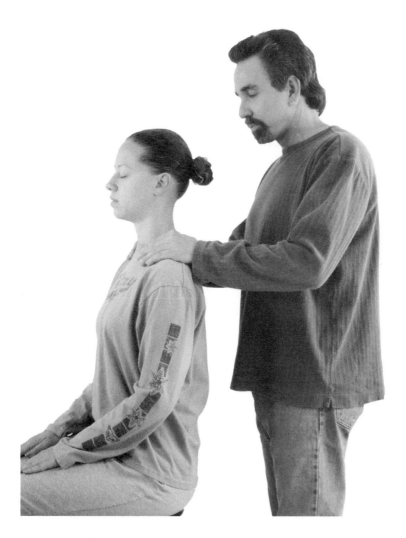

4. I place my hands on the shoulders and give a blessing which is, "We are both blessed by this process."

5. I move to the front, and then ask the person to breathe deeply and slowly while opening their eyes. *The Reiki Psychic Attunement is complete.*

"However many holy words you read, however many you speak, what good will they do if you do not act upon them?"

-Buddha

"The secret of health for both mind and body is not to mourn for the past, nor to worry about the future, but to live the present moment wisely and earnestly."

-Buddha

Chapter Nine

Reiki Healing Attunement

The Reiki Healing Attunement will help heal emotional, mental, physical and spiritual issues. The attunement does that by bringing in Reiki for specific healing, and then helps clear any blockages where the healing needs to occur. This attunement can be taken many times for reinforcement or when a new issue needs to be healed.

This Reiki Attunement is given for specific healing only and does not attune the person to any Reiki Level because symbols are not placed in the hands, which sometimes is a concern of the person receiving it.

This attunement can only be performed by a Reiki Master and should be done in private. There is a requirement in this attunement; the person receiving it has to choose what he or she needs healed. They can only choose one healing issue per attunement. They *must* hold this issue in their mind throughout the attunement. The person does not have to divulge the healing issue to the Reiki Master giving the attunement. If another issue(s) needs to be healed, another attunement is required.

The following are the instructions for the Reiki Healing Attunement. When I give the attunement I work in three areas, the Heart, Throat and Crown Chakras. You prepare the same way as with the other attunements, except your intent is to give a Healing Attunement. Again, before the session the person must decide what issue they would like healed, and keep it in their mind throughout the attunement. The person keeps their hands in their lap.

Reiki Healing Attunement

1st part from the back

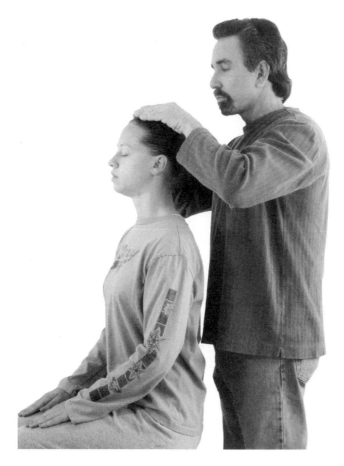

1. I place both hands on top of the head of the person, meditating for 15 to 30 seconds to start the Reiki connection with the person.

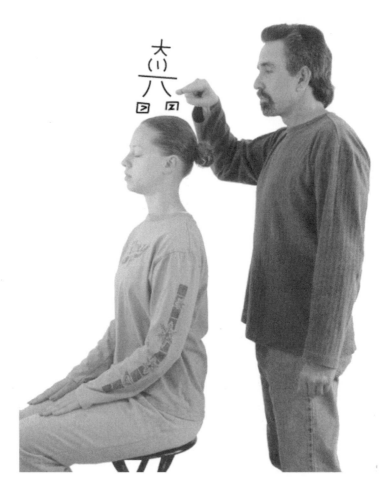

2. I draw the Master Symbol in the air on top of the head (Crown Chakra) and visualize it going down into the head past the Throat Chakra, lodging into the Heart Chakra. While this is being done, I state the symbol's name silently one time then state silently, "All blockages are now cleared and released."

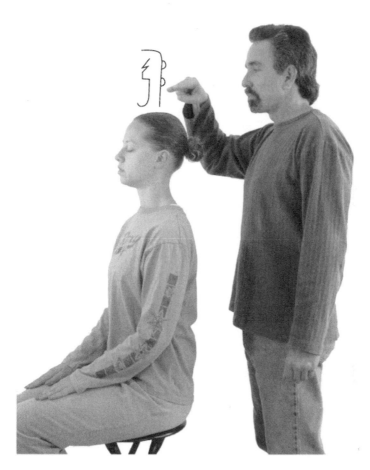

3. I draw the Mental/Emotional Symbol in the air on top of the head (Crown Chakra) and visualize it going down into the head past the Throat Chakra, lodging into the Heart Chakra. While this is being done, I state the symbol's name silently one time then state silently, "All blockages are now cleared and released."

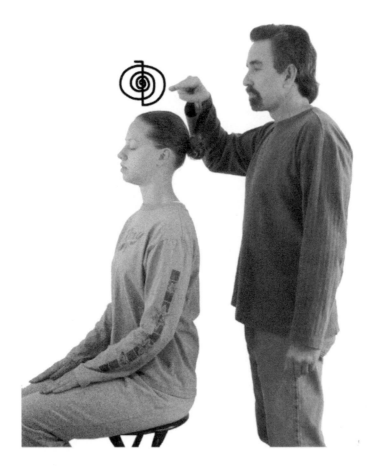

4. I draw the Power Symbol in the air on top of the head (Crown Chakra) and visualize it going down into the head past the Throat Chakra, lodging into the Heart Chakra. While this is being done, I state the symbol's name silently one time then state silently, "All blockages are now cleared and released."

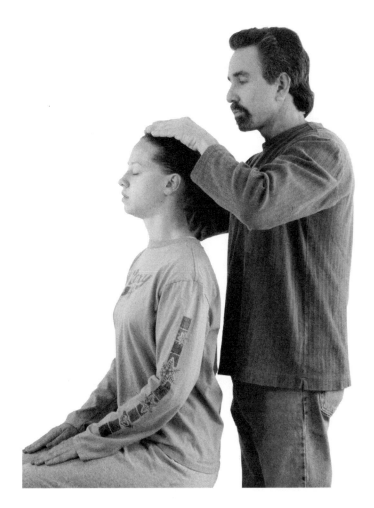

5. I then place both hands together, palms down over the Crown Chakra and channel Reiki for a few minutes. While doing this, I visualize Reiki flowing through the Crown, Throat and Heart Chakras all the way down the body and out the feet into the earth. When I am done with this, I move to the front.

2nd Part from the front

1. I am at the front.

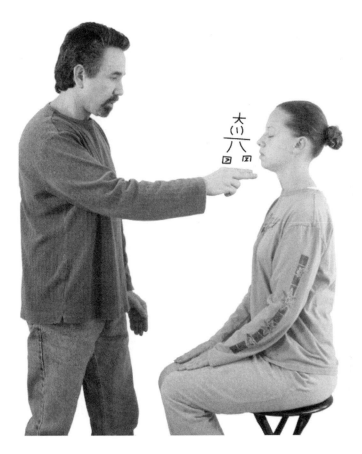

2. I draw the Master Symbol in the air in front of the Throat Chakra and visualize it going into and lodging in the middle of the Throat Chakra. While this is being done, the symbol's name is said silently one time.

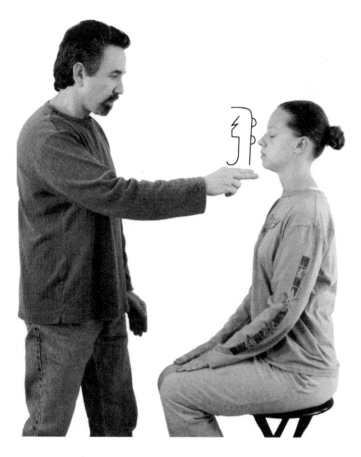

3. I draw the Mental/Emotional Symbol in the air in front of the Throat Chakra and visualize it going into and lodging in the middle of the Throat Chakra. While this is being done, the symbol's name is said silently one time.

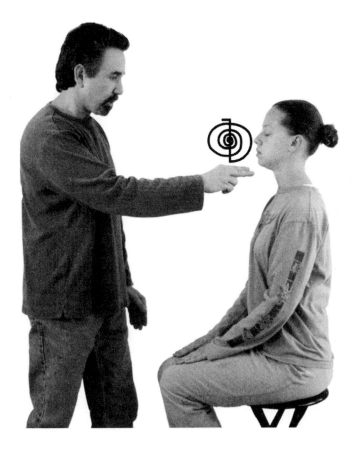

4. I draw the Power Symbol in the air in front of the Throat Chakra and visualize it going into and lodging in the middle of the Throat Chakra. While this is being done, the symbol's name is said silently one time.

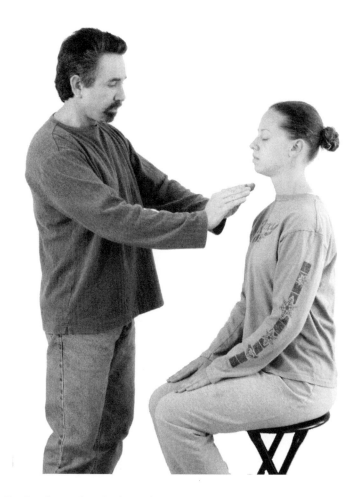

5. I place both hands open palms facing the Throat Chakra and Heart Chakra (they do not have to touch the body) and I channel Reiki for a few minutes to both areas. While channeling the Reiki I state silently, "The healing issue held in this person's thoughts is now being healed." When I am done, I move to the back.

3rd Part from the back

1. I am at the back

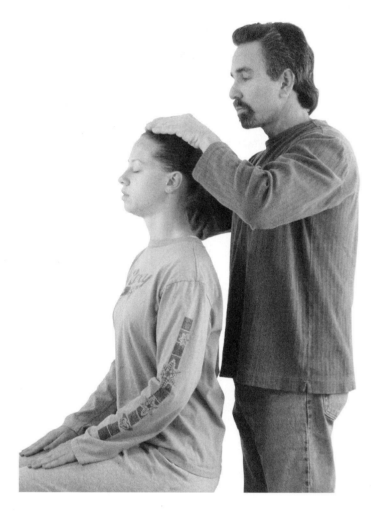

2. I place my hands on the Crown Chakra and channel Reiki for a minute. Then I place an affirmation into the Crown Chakra by saying silently three times, "The healing issue held in this person's thoughts will be healed for their Highest Good."

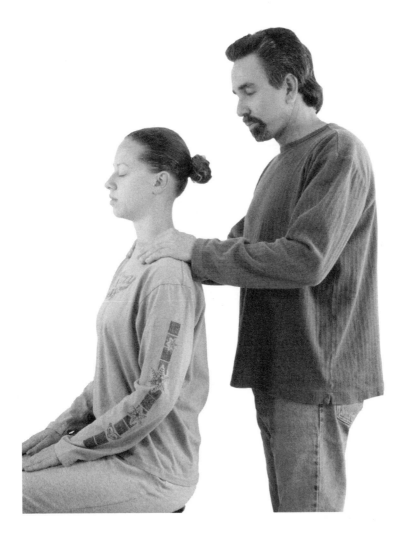

3. I place my hands on the shoulders and give a blessing which is, "We are both blessed by this process."

4. I move to the front, and then ask the person to breathe deeply and slowly while opening their eyes. *The Reiki Healing Attunement is complete.*

"Neither fire nor wind, birth nor death can erase our good deeds."

-Buddha

"To be idle is a short road to death and to be diligent is a way of life; foolish people are idle, wise people are diligent."

-Buddha

Chapter Ten

Contacting Spirits With Reiki

This chapter is about how to contact spirits and departed loved ones with Reiki. I have a video program entitled "How to Contact Spirits, Angels and Departed Love Ones" a step-by step guide that is for everybody. I am going to show you how to include Reiki in the process, which will enable the contact to manifest faster and clearer. Using Reiki will also make you more open and receptive to contact from the other side.

I personally do not recommend trying to contact the other side for fun or games, especially if you do not take the right precautions. An unpleasant experience can manifest during the contact. Even professional mediums bring forth the wrong contacts at times, it just happens. But they know how to protect themselves and their clients when this occurs.

I feel there are good reasons and appropriate times to make spiritual contact. Sometimes people need help in acquiring closure to heal and move on in life when their loved ones or friends have crossed over.

Closure might be difficult for some people because they did not get a chance to say good-bye, if the crossing was sudden. It could be the need to heal an argument they feel guilty about that happened when the person was alive. Or it could be the need to receive forgiveness, an answer to a question they never had a chance to ask, or maybe they just want to know that the person is OK. There can be many personal reasons that closure is difficult for some people.

This process is not for everyone nor does everyone have a dilemma with closure or even desire to have a spiritual contact with the other side. You will find a majority of the time when the contact is made once or twice for these people, they never have the need to do it again. They have the closure they seek and can heal and move forward.

So, as a Reiki Healer you can expect on occasion to be asked to contact the other side by a client, family, friends or students. When that happens, this chapter will help guide you. One last caveat: I advise only contacting loved ones and/or friends that have crossed over by closely following the guidelines presented in this chapter. If you do this, you will never have a problem.

Spirits

I believe spirits can be Angels, or people who have died and crossed over to the other side. But, there is a difference between the two. Angels have never had a human form on earth and are here to help, protect and guide us. It is said we all have at least one Guardian Angel. People who have died and crossed over have been in human form. There is a belief that they were and still are on a learning path and they can also help and guide us when contacted.

A Spiritual Connection

A spiritual connection is when you go to a higher state of awareness. You are then receptive to spirits and are able to communicate with them. You will not be tired or asleep, but you will be in an altered state of awareness. It's this state of awareness that you are going to enhance with the use of Reiki.

Why Contact Spirits?

As previously mentioned, people want to make spiritual contact for many different reasons. It can be for guidance, closure, healing, giving and receiving messages, finding lost objects or it could be as simple as saying hello or good-bye. Spirits can help you in all areas of your life.

Spirit Contact

At various times throughout our lives spirits do contact us. It's a matter of being aware, listening, seeing and understanding the signs of communication. Once you open up your spiritual connection, you will start becoming more aware of these contacts. You will be able to understand and accept the information and guidance to help you in your life. What you will learn here is how to intentionally contact spirits through a session.

How Do Spirits Communicate?

Spirits communicate through intuition, sound, touch, voices, color, hunches, dé jà vu, thoughts, symbols, visions, dreams, feelings, smells, writing and other creative ways. A small percentage of the times they may even appear in front of you. Spirits will contact you by one of the many different ways mentioned or by a combination of them. This creates what I refer to as an *experience*.

This experience can happen with other people around, but you will be the only person to witness it. Or, it can happen and many people will experience it at the same time.

Once you become aware of the way you personally receive communication from spirits, that's usually the way you will receive it from then on.

Receiving Answers and Messages

You will always receive answers and information in some form when you make spiritual contact. The challenge is to be aware of and understand it. Sometimes you will instantly understand what is being sent to you. This will happen more often as you develop your awareness and understanding. However, this is a process that must be developed with practice, patience and at your own pace. You will always make contact; it's just a matter of being aware you were contacted in return and understanding what was sent.

Understanding Your Answers and Messages

I have explained to you the many different ways you receive messages and answers when you make spiritual contact. This information is filtered through your own belief system for your interpretation and understanding. Spirits are aware of this and communicate with you in the way your belief system will be able to understand.

This understanding and interpretation of the messages and answers will arrive as a thought, a picture or even a voice that will just float up to your conscious mind or awareness. You will receive this during and right after a session or through the technique that will be shown later on.

Spirit Personality

Spirits have personalities. You will discover Angels will have their own unique personalities when they communicate with you. When you contact spirits of people who have died and crossed over, you will find they still have their same personality, including unique quirks and sense of humor.

Prayer & Meditation

In prayer, usually you are asking for something. In

meditation you are listening for the answer or guidance. In contacting spirits you use a combination of both.

Contacting Pet Spirits

You can contact pets that have died and crossed over. You do it through the same process that you will learn in this chapter. Pet spirits usually communicate to you through your thoughts and feelings and have been known to appear during a session.

Increased Awareness

Once you start contacting spirits your awareness will keep increasing and expanding in all levels of your life. On occasion, you will discover spirits are sending you messages in your everyday life. Once you open up the spiritual connection your intuition and hunches will become stronger and you will have the confidence to act on them.

Spiritual Connection in a Different Place

Sometimes when you have a spiritual connection you will be taken to a different place other than the room you are in. It could be an out of body experience or you will just feel, sense, or see yourself in this different place. Don't be alarmed. Just flow with it and receive the information and messages sent. Most of the time you will be contacted where you are.

Session-Experience-Understanding

When you are in the process of contacting a spirit I call it a "*session*." When you have contact with a spirit I call that an "*experience*." Because when you are being contacted, you are experiencing the way you receive the information sent through sound, visions, feelings, smell etc. When I refer to receiving an "*understanding*" of the contact, it means just that, understanding what was sent.

What to do During a Spiritual Connection

During a session, when you are receiving information and messages sent from spirits, it is extremely important never to analyze or judge. Just witness and experience it. I know this will be hard at first for some people and it will take practice. If you start to analyze or judge as the information arrives, you will soon get stuck and miss the rest of the information and message. Or it will just stop flowing altogether.

This usually happens in your first sessions. If this does occur, don't get discouraged. You will just have to start over from the beginning or do it another day.

Now here's the exception, if you hear or see a spirit, you must be calm. Should you become alarmed or panic, there's a good chance the contact will be lost. You can talk to the spirit out loud or silently with any question you may have. After you ask a question, wait for an answer before you ask another. Never ask more than one question at a time. If you ask a question and there is no response, just listen and watch.

Crying & Laughing

On rare occasions when you are in a session you may become emotional and have the urge to cry or perhaps laugh. If this happens don't suppress it. Usually it will not last long. This is part of a healing and cleansing process your spirits are guiding you through. When you are done just continue with the session. If you feel the need, you can stop the session and do it another day.

Stopping a Session

You can always stop your session at any point without any problems. You just open your eyes, touch your forehead with one hand, then rub your hands together briefly, and take several deep breaths and you are back. I always recommend if you stop a session, do not do another for 24 hours.

Step-by-Step

I always recommend if possible for those wishing to contact spirits, to take a Psychic Attunement some time in your life. Though not mandatory, it will help with your connections.

Please use your intuition and guidance and be flexible within the following guidelines. You might have to adjust and change them for your circumstances and situations. For example you might have a whole family or group in one session. And they might want only you to make contact. But, one in the group might receive contact also. Or the whole group may want to receive contact or maybe just a few. You might want to give Reiki to the people before or after the session. There are many situations that can arise, the key is to be fluid and do what you feel is right. The following guidelines will help with that.

The Spiritual Portal

Before you start any spiritual connections, you should open your spiritual portal. There is a prayer meditation that is simple but very effective for opening it. You only have to do it once because after that you will open and close it each time during a session by touching your hand to your forehead. If you have a person(s) you are going to do a session with, you should open their portal before any sessions. If they do not want to open the portal for any reason, that is OK, yours will be open for the session.

Allow 10 to 15 minutes for the process and again you only need to do it once. It is very simple. To open it, get into a meditative state for 5 minutes, then state the following prayer/meditation. You can record, read or memorize it and say it silently or out loud. Then meditate on the words for another 5 minutes. You will then be attuned for opening and closing your spiritual portal during sessions.

Opening The Spiritual Portal

◆ Get in a relaxed meditative state for 5 minutes. Then state the following:

The Prayer / Meditation

I ask that my spiritual portal be cleared and opened for spiritual connections for my highest good. That this expanding and opening of my spiritual portal only allow spirits for my highest good to come forth. I ask that I will be guided and protected during my spiritual contact and have contact only with spirits that I seek for information and guidance. That I receive this information with clarity and understanding in a form I can understand. I ask that this spiritual portal be open each time I touch my forehead with my right hand before spiritual contact and for the portal to be closed when I touch my forehead again after the contact is over. So it is.

◆ Meditate on the words for 5 minutes and it is done.

How I Prepare for a Session

◆ Before each contact I clear and protect the room where the session will take place. I also clear and protect myself with Reiki.

◆ I clear my mind of any distractions so that I am in an open and receptive mood.

◆ I make sure the room is calm and quiet so I will not be disturbed. I turn off phones and pagers. You can have candles or low lights and maybe burn incense if you like. You can play soothing music of your choice.

◆ If there is more than one person in a session, have everybody sit around the same table. Or, if you are on the floor make a circle. One person can say the prayer (this prayer is explained later) or everybody can say it silently to themselves. Wear comfortable, loose clothes. A session can get warm during a contact.

◆ I like to have in the room if possible, a picture, jewelry, clothes item or any small possession of the spirit being contacted. This can be set on the table or in front of you on the floor. If you don't have any items, that's OK. But I find if you do have articles it makes the spiritual connection stronger.

◆ I believe in keeping every session simple. Ask and/or send only a few messages each session. Too many messages coming and going will be confusing for both sides, and quality will be lost in the connection.

◆ Have a note pad and pencil or pen available. Write down on the pad the name of the spirit you want to contact. For example, if you are contacting your uncle Stan Smith, you write down Stan Smith. I strongly recommend not contacting spirits unless they are loved ones or friends. But, if you choose not to heed this advice, and you are just contacting the other side, then write on the pad, the spirit for my highest good. This will ensure only a spirit for your highest good will come through.

♦ Another important point is to only contact one spirit at a time. Now on occasion, a loved one or friend will make contact that was not on the pad. If that happens, receive the information and or/message because most of the time it pertains to your reason for contact. During the next session you can contact the spirit's name you originally wrote down and the spirit should come through.

♦ Once you have written down the name of the spirit you want to contact, write down the question and or message you want to send. For example, "Stan, I am sorry I was not there for you, do you forgive me?" Or "Stan are you OK?" You can write any message or question that you personally want. If you do not have a question or message for this spirit you would write, "Stan Smith please send me information for my (our) highest good."

♦ This pad will be placed in front of you. It does not matter how many people are in a session, only one pad is needed. Of course the few questions and messages have to be decided on and that is usually before the session. On the back of the pad that has the writing, I actually draw all four Reiki Symbols. If you have only been attuned to three, then draw all three. They do not have to be large and can be placed in an area on the back of the pad.

Prayer

Each time I contact spirits I say a prayer before the session begins. The prayer has to have certain elements in it. The prayer can be in your own words and can include whatever you feel intuitively you should say. It can be said out loud or silently. Somewhere in the prayer the following must be included:

1. Ask your source, god, higher power or whatever your belief, for your protection and well being during this session
2. Ask for white or a golden healing light to surround you and fill the room
3. Ask for wisdom and guidance through this session
4. Ask that this session will be only for your highest good

Example of a Basic Prayer

I ask my source for my protection and well-being during this session. I ask for a white healing light to surround me and fill the room. I ask for wisdom and guidance and that this session will be only for my highest good.

After the Contact

After the session you might have an immediate understanding of the information sent. If there are people in the session, share it with them. Or the person(s) at the session might have received the

265

information themselves. Each session will be unique and unfold differently. Either way this information should be shared and discussed with everybody present.

When you first start making spiritual contact, or even when you are experienced, you may not have an immediate understanding of the information that was sent. If this happens, it's very important that you write down or draw everything that you experienced during the session at the end of the session. You and /or the person(s) present can do this. You can elaborate as much as you feel necessary in your writing or it can be simply stated. Drawings can be very simple or detailed. It can also be a combination of both. For example: you saw a tall waterfall, heard a bell, felt hot, and then saw the color purple turn into a beautiful rainbow. You could just write this down in a list, or you could draw the waterfall, bell and rainbow and write the rest of the experience. It is however you want to do it. Even if you just saw black and felt light headed, write it down. In spiritual connections, everything has a meaning for the person it was intended for. Again you can do this or everyone that is present can participate. This is up to you, the person(s) involved and what works best for the session.

When the writing and drawing are complete, the information can be shared and everybody can then compare notes and discuss their experience. After that, if there isn't a clear understanding of the information received, keep the notes. At the end of the chapter I will show you a method for receiving an understanding of the contact experience.

Guide Lines for Contacting Spirits

Next are the guidelines I use for contacting spirits. Study them many times before you actually do a session. It's very important to do the steps in sequence, unless otherwise guided by your intuition.

♦   Clear the room with Reiki. Then draw as many Reiki Symbols as you are attuned to in the middle of the room. This will ensure they are there for the session.

♦   Ground and protect yourself with Reiki.

♦   Have the room ready and the right atmosphere as explained before.

♦   Prepare mentally by clearing your mind of all thoughts not related to the session.

♦   If you have items of the spirit you are going to contact, place them in front of you. That could be on a table or on the floor. Draw the Long Distance Symbol over these items.

♦   Place your notepad in front of you with the names of the spirit you want to contact and the messages and/or questions you want answered. The note pad should be prepared before the session. But, it can be done at this time. Make sure you draw all the Reiki Symbols you have been attuned to on the back of this page. I recommend actually drawing them with a pencil or pen.

◆ Have everybody present put their hands palms up in their lap and do the following steps:

◆ Close eyes.

◆ Say the prayer with the four elements silently or out loud. One person or all can do this.

◆ Pause for a minute or so.

◆ Start breathing deeply and slowly. Just focus on your breath going in and out of your physical body. Do this for about three to five minutes. Or until you feel ready to go to the next step. If you are leading the session, it is up to you when to move on.

◆ Touch your forehead with your right hand to activate your spiritual portal. Keep your hand there for a few seconds. Then put your hand back down in the open palm position. If there are other people in the session, they will do the same unless their spiritual portal has not been cleared and opened.

◆ Be calm and wait, your spiritual connection has begun.

◆ The messages and information you will receive during this time will be in the form of spirits communicating to you as explained earlier in the chapter. What you are experiencing during this time is the "*contact*." The experience might manifest slow or fast and it might be brief or last a while. Each session will be different. There is not a set time. Five minutes can seem like an hour, an hour can seem like five minutes. You will find your perception of time will be distorted during the session.

♦ When your experience has stopped or you sense the spirit has left, the contact is over and it's time to come back. Again there is no set time on this, but, if you are doing this by yourself, you will feel and sense when it is over. And the same is true if there are people present. You are guiding the session and you will know when it is over and it will be up to you to bring it to a close.

♦ Once it is over, take several deep breaths and thank the spirit for coming. Touch your forehead with your right hand to close the spiritual connection, then rub both hands together for a few seconds and slowly open your eyes. If other people are present they will do the same.

♦ Relax for a few moments, if you or another person received information that you understand, share what you received. If there was not a clear understanding write down or draw what you experienced. Then review it with the people present to see if there is now any clarity in what was experienced. It is a good idea even if you understand what was sent, to write down and draw your experience and keep it for future reference.

♦ If you did not understand what was experienced

after drawing and writing down the experience and sharing it, use the following process to receive it.

Receive an Understanding of the Contact

The following steps are the process for acquiring an understanding of a contact if it was not understood at the end of the session.

♦ On the first night after the session before you go to bed, read and review the notes and/or drawings from the session. This process has to be started on the first night for it to be effective. Draw the Master (if you are a Master) Power and Long Distance Symbols in front of your bed. Then ask the spirit from which the information came for an understanding of it. This can be done out loud or silently. Then go to bed. It is that simple. Now if the person(s) that were in this session are not Reiki attuned, they would do the same process with the exception of the symbols over the bed.

♦ You must do this every night for the next 15 days. You will receive an understanding sometime over the course of those next 15 days. It might come in day three or on the fifteenth day. Once you receive your understanding you can stop the process.

♦ Spirits will help you understand the information in your dream-state where your conscious mind will not interfere. The key is to remember it.

♦ You might awaken in the middle of the night with the understanding, or you might receive it when you

270

awake the next morning. It may float up to your conscious mind anytime and anywhere over the next fifteen days or nights. I recommend keeping a pad and pen by your bed. If you awake in the middle of the night or in the morning with the information, write it down right away. Also during the day if you receive information, write it down as soon as you can. At times, people did not write the information down, and it was lost. Especially in the middle of the night this can happen, the information is lost upon awakening.

Once you receive the information, you can contact the person(s) requesting it, unless it was for yourself. If more than one person is doing the process, I recommend meeting after 15 days to share the information that was acquired. On occasion, the information will be given in different parts to the people involved. Or one person will only receive the information in the group. This can be determined at the meeting after 15 days.

Once you reach a higher spiritual level, you will be able to understand the messages and answers from spirits during or right after a session. Reaching that higher level comes with time, practice, patience and experience. I wish you peace and light in all your spiritual connections.

"Let us rise up and be thankful, for if we didn't learn a lot today, at least we learned a little, and if we didn't learn a little, at least we didn't get sick, and if we got sick, at least we didn't die, so, let us all be thankful."

- Buddha

Chapter Eleven

Beaming and Scanning

There are several very effective techniques that Reiki Masters and Practitioners can use in their Reiki sessions. They include Beaming and Scanning. I personally believe the ideal Reiki session has a combination of both.

Beaming is a process that can channel Reiki to each of the four bodies (mental, physical, emotional and spiritual) at once.

Scanning is locating the specific areas in the bodies that have a problem, and need extra Reiki. If a person comes in with a specific ailment you want to treat that area, but usually that area is only the symptom. By Scanning you should be able to find the area that is the root cause of the symptom. At the very least, you will be able to detect areas that need healing before they get serious.

Beaming

There are several ways Beaming can be done. One way is to Beam at the start of the Reiki session, or at the end of a session. Some Reiki Masters and practitioners make a habit of Beaming every Reiki session. It usually only takes a few minutes, but the results are worth it. The other way is to do a session of just Beaming, which will take longer. This is done when you sense there is a major need for extra Reiki throughout the four bodies. Beaming Reiki is very effective in cleansing and healing the mental, emotional and spiritual bodies by releasing blockages and Psychic Debris clinging to them.

To Beam, have the person sit or lay in a relaxed position. I usually do it with the person in a seated position. I position myself facing the person and standing about 6-8 feet away. I draw all four Reiki Symbols in the air in front of me, three symbols if 2nd Level and none if 1st Level. I hold my hands open, palms toward the person. Then I Beam the Reiki over the person for 1-2 minutes or until I sense it is enough. If it is just a Beaming session, I Beam for at least 5-10 minutes or until I sense it is enough. While Beaming the Reiki I visualize it spreading over the whole person like a large beam of golden or white light.

To beam, I position myself facing the person and standing about 6-8 feet away.

Scanning

As a Reiki Practitioner or Master your Palm Chakras are open from the attunements you have received. You are now used to the feeling of the Reiki flowing through them. But, Scanning is a process where you use your Palm Chakras not to channel Reiki, but to detect problem areas that need extra Reiki. With Scanning you go over (scan) a person's body with your open Palm Chakras to detect areas that need healing and/or extra Reiki. This process can detect problems in the energy field of all four bodies: the physical, mental, emotional and spiritual.

Scanning is performed on others, but can also be done on yourself. The more scanning you do, the more sensitive your Palm Chakras will become in detecting problem areas that require Reiki.

How to Scan

Before you scan, draw the Power Symbol and Master Symbol (if you are a Master) in the palms of both hands. It is usually easier to scan if the person is lying down, but they can be seated.

When scanning you can use one hand or two (I use two), and you have your palms about 4 inches off the person's body. You can start at the top of the person's body or at the feet. Slowly move the palms over the body and you will start to feel and sense how this person's energy feels. If you

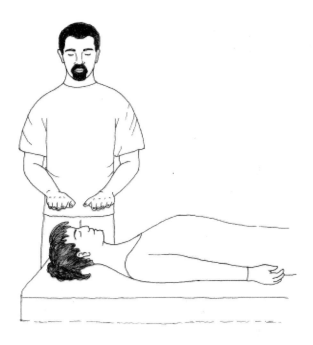

When scanning you can use one hand or two (I use two), with your palms about 4 inches off the person's body.

feel a change--it could be heat, cold, no energy, a strange vibration, or any irregularity--stop there.

You then take one hand and move it up and down in that area until you find the level where it is most intense. This could be as high as 12-16 inches.

Then channel Reiki (with both hands) from that level, to that area. You stop giving Reiki when you feel the area is balanced and/or had enough Reiki. This usually takes a few minutes.

Again, this is very important. The reason you find the right level before you give Reiki is the problem might be in the spiritual, mental or emotional body. If you channel at a lower level you will miss the area that needs it the most.

Once you are done with an area you have found that needs Reiki, continue Scanning down the front of the body and if you detect any disturbance in another area, do the same process and so on. When you are done with the front side of the person, you repeat it on the backside. The amount of time needed for a Scanning session of course, depends on how many areas you detect that need Reiki.

"What we think, we become."

-Buddha

"Holding onto anger is like grasping a hot coal with the intent of throwing it at someone else; you are the one getting burned."

-Buddha

Chapter Twelve

Antahkarana

Antahkarana - Ancient Symbol Of Healing

I was shown by a Reiki Master years ago a very unique and potent symbol that was used in China and Tibet for thousands of years. It was used in meditation and healing rituals by Tibetan Monks. The symbol is referred to as Antahkarana.

The symbol has been passed down from a few select Tibetan Monks to a small number of people and Reiki Masters throughout the years. It has been kept relatively secret for centuries and used to enhance healing by only a few.

The Antahkarana is a multi-dimensional symbol. From one angle it looks two dimensional, with the appearance of three sevens. From another angle it looks like a three dimensional cube. It is also drawn two ways. One way is labeled the female version and the other the male version.

It is no coincidence that the symbol looks like the Swastika. It is known the Hitler believed in and was a student of the occult and did rituals for his evil goals.[1] Most likely he took this healing symbol and altered it for his own purposes, which eventually backfired. But, when the symbol is used and drawn the way it was intended, only healing energy can be generated from it.

How To Use It

The symbol usually is meditated on with the eyes open for healing. It has also been known to produce altered states with visions and connecting a person to a higher level of awareness when meditating on it.

I personally do not use this symbol, but many people do and experience positive healing results. Let your intuition guide you on using this symbol (either version) or just experiment with it. You can make a copy of both symbols for your own use.

[1] **Spear of Destiny**" by Trevor Ravenscroft
Published by Samuel Weiser, 1987, ISBN: 0877285470

Male Antahkarana

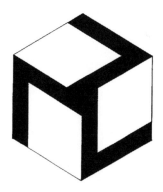

Female Antahkarana

"Do not overrate what you have received, nor envy others. He who envies others does not obtain peace of mind."

-Buddha

Chapter Thirteen

Reiki Psychic Surgery

The majority of the time Reiki Attunements and Sessions are successful in removing and clearing Psychic Debris. But, on occasion you will have a person with a stubborn blockage caused by Psychic Debris. I use Reiki Psychic Surgery in these situations. The majority of the time the surgery is done in the physical body, but on rare occasions, I might have to work on one of the other three bodies (emotional, mental spiritual) with these blockages.

There are a few other techniques and methods used and taught for Psychic Surgery. Some are more complicated than others, but they will all work. I will explain the method I use successfully.

During a surgery session you will be interacting with the person by asking questions, receiving answers and guiding them. They must be made aware of this and want to cooperate during the session. Before the session you prepare the person by telling them you will ask questions during it and they should respond with the first information that comes to their mind. If nothing comes to their mind when they are asked a question, they have to then imagine what the answer is. Explain they do not have to worry about the answer being wrong if they have to imagine it. Whatever they imagine is the right information for the surgery. If for some reason the person cannot even imagine an answer to one of your questions, the surgery cannot be done. Reschedule for another day and try again.

Prepare for Surgery

◆ Prepare and protect yourself the same way as you do for Reiki Attunements and sessions.

◆ Have the person sit comfortably in a chair.

◆ Explain to the person receiving the surgery about answering questions and the process. Answer any questions they might have.

◆ Have the person close their eyes, clear their mind and breathe deeply and relax for a few minutes before you start the surgery. You can guide them in this relaxation if you like.

◆ Once the person is relaxed, ask them to scan their body from head to toe with their mind to see where the blockage is. Then wait until you receive an answer. For example, the answer might be they feel the blockage is in the heart or throat. If a person is having a hard time finding the blockage, you then ask them just to imagine or guess where it is. Whatever they guess or imagine, that is the area you will work with. It might take a while for them to find the area with the blockage, but that is very rare.

◆ Once you have established the location of the blockage, you ask the following questions to determine if you will proceed or not. Ask the person if they are ready to have the blockage removed, and wait for the answer. If the answer is yes, then continue with the surgery. If they answer no, ask if they will be willing to have a portion of it removed. If they answer yes, move to the next step. If they answer no (it does happen), I recommend just doing a Reiki session. You can continue, but it will be difficult if not impossible to have a successful surgery. Just schedule another session and hopefully they will be ready at that time. There can be many different reasons for a person not wanting the surgery at that time and I do not analyze or worry about it. Sometimes it takes a while before they are willing to have the blockage removed. Have patience and work with the person until they are ready.

Now that you know the person is willing to have at least part of the blockage removed, continue with the following questions. If they cannot answer a question, you ask them to imagine or guess an answer. You must receive an answer to a question before you move to the next.

Questions:

- *How long has the blockage been there?*

- *How big is it?*

- *What color is it?*

- *How much does it weigh?*

- *Does it have a smell, if so what does it smell like?*

Once you have asked the questions above, you and the person will know everything about this blockage and are now ready to remove it. If the person had stated earlier that the whole blockage can be removed, then proceed to the surgery. If it was stated they only wanted a part removed, you have to ask and establish how much of it you can remove. Once you get the answer (example, they say half of it), you move forward to the surgery.

Performing the Surgery

◆ Stand about two to three feet in front of the area where the blockage is located in the person.

◆ Focus your eyes on the area, and visualize the complete blockage as it was described; weight, size, color, etc.

◆ Take your right Palm Chakra and have it facing the area where the blockage is located.

◆ Use your intent and start channeling Reiki like a focused laser beam from your Palm Chakra. By moving your right palm you are able to direct this beam where you want it to go. Now, with your right palm directing this focused laser of Reiki, start moving the beam around the boundaries of the blockage and keep circling it closer towards the center of it. While this beam is hitting the blockage, visualize and intend for it to be dissolved and destroyed, just like a laser would. Keep circling the beam towards the center of the blockage until it is completely dissolved and destroyed. The length of time for the surgery will depend on its size. If you are only removing a portion of the blockage, you do the same process, but only remove the portion decided upon.

◆ Once you are done dissolving the Psychic Debris, ask the person to scan the area with their mind to see if any blockage remains. Most of the time it will be completely gone. But, when they scan, if they detect a portion left, you ask how much and where, and do additional surgery. You then ask them to check again. On rare occasions you might have to do surgery on the blockage several times to completely dissolve it.

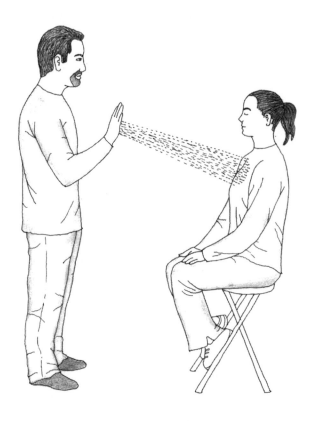

Take your right Palm Chakra and have it facing the area where the blockage is located.

In all Psychic Surgery the following steps are very important and are left out in some teachings. There is now a void in the person's body from dissolving and removing the blockage or part of it.

◆ In the void you place the Power Symbol and the Mental/Emotional Symbol. You do this by drawing them over the area where the blockage was.

◆ Next have the person and yourself simultaneously visualize sending and filling this void left by the surgery with a golden, sticky light, until it is completely filled. This should only take a few minutes.

◆ When this is done, have the person scan the area with their mind to make sure the void is filled. If it is, do the last step. If the person detects an area that is not filled, repeat the process. Do the process as many times as it takes, until the person has a scan with the void completely filled.

◆ When the void is filled, just have the person relax for a few minutes, then open their eyes and the surgery is done.

◆ Do your normal cleansing and protection after a session.

291

"Words have the power to both destroy and heal. When words are both true and kind, they can change our world."

-Buddha

Index

Selected Bibliography

Haberky,H. *Hawayo Takata's Story.* Archedigm Publications. 1990 ISBN 0-944135-06-04

Brown, F. *Living Reiki Takata's Teachings.* LifeRythm 1992 ISBN 0-940795-10-8

Petter, F. *The Original Reiki Handbook of Dr. Mikao Usui.* Lotus Press 1999 ISBN 0-914955-57-8

Petter, F. *Reiki Fire.* Lotus Press 1997 ISBN 0-914955-5-0

Borang, K. *Principles of Reiki.* Thorsons 1997 ISBN 0-7225-3406-X

Baginski, B. & Sharamon, S. *Reiki Universal Life Energy.* LifeRythm 1985 ISBN 0-940795-02-7

Waites, B. & Naharo M. *Reiki a Practical Guide* Astrolog Publishing 1998 ISBN 965-494-046-9

Lubeck, W. *Reiki Way of the Heart* Lotus Light 1996 ISBN 0-941524-91-4

Morris, J. *Reiki Hands That Heal* 1996 ISBN 1-888196-05-x

Nevius, S. & Arnold L. *The Reiki Handbook* PSI Press 1982 0-9625500-1-9

Rowland, A. *Traditional Reiki For Our Times* Healing Arts Press 1998 ISBN 0-89281-777-1

More of what people are saying...

-I have watched the video several times with different experiences. The first time I seemed to feel a rush--the air seemed to move towards me & I saw different colors; I definitely felt different, like I had experienced something. Next I saw the background moving while watching the crystal. I remember one other important experience from the first time I watched the video--I saw symbols coming from the left hand side of the screen from the bottom to the top then swirling outward. I thought these symbols were actually on the video. But when I watched the video the next few times, I realized they weren't on it. I recommend this video to people interested in trying Reiki. *B. N.*

-Last night I sat with your Master Attunement tape and I commend you. The attunement was very very powerful and I had the "Reiki high" for hours afterwards. The lady that I had received a master attunement before did the attunement and that's about it. There wasn't a lot of information given as far as how to use the symbol and pass attunements. This morning I called all of my Reiki Master friends and told them that they must get your tape! I was taught the non-traditional symbol in Diane Stein's book and I would like to work with the traditional symbol that you show. *D.Z.*

-I did not feel that much the first time I did the attunement, but woke up the next morning full of energy and enthusiasm for living. I have felt much more energetic and optimistic about life since then. With repeated viewings, I have started to see some color in the crystal and feel definite heat. I have felt a huge increase in my healing power after viewing these videos, and have experienced healing of the discomfort in my hip. With this video, using the Reiki energy, I am able to channel greater amounts of energy without the discomfort. I believe this is either because the blockage has been cleared up, or because the energy is powerful and gentle at the same time, or both. *W.S.*

-I took both 2nd Level and the Master Attunement after getting Reiki 1st Level elsewhere. I noticed a connection right away upon seeing Steve's image. I feel the Reiki much stronger now. I ended up buying 1st Level Reiki and the Psychic Attunement and will be showing them to my family members. I now have access too much needed but often difficult to get attunements. Thank you Steve! *R.W.*

-I highly recommend this video. It has been a wealth of knowledge and guidance on my spiritual journey. Steve Murray's delivery is very to the point, and very informative. He has a strong presence and gets his message to the student without convolution. *N.A.*

-The first two times I took the attunement I maybe noticed a little change in my awareness, if that. The third time WOW!...my awareness went to a higher level and i started having dreams that gave me information I needed. Great program. *J.M.*

-I ordered your Reiki I & II videos a few weeks ago and just now found some time to watch the first one. I am already a level II practitioner and wanted to buy your videos for reinforcement. I just wanted to let you know that I definitely felt my energy became stronger during and after the attunement. It really works! *K.C.*

-I have taken the Healing Attunement two or three times. It has helped me to experience a feeling of peace regarding the problems I worked on, and the faith that a higher power will help guide events, my thoughts and my emotions in such a way that the problems will be healed. When I watch this video, I see colors in the crystal. I feel as if I become one with the crystal, and that my problems are being surrounded with light and healed. I also feel healing heat in my body as soon as the video starts playing, even before the actual attunement begins. This program really works. *F.M.*

-I was already a 2nd Level, but this attunement reinforced my Reiki. Plus it filled in the blanks for me in using the Long Distance Symbol. And it gave me tips for using the other two Reiki symbols. *S.G.*

-The three videos gave me really wonderful experiences, made me happier than ever before. I will share these beautiful & wonderful videos. *A.T.K.*

-I am witness that each individual can have different profound experiences each and every time the attunement is taken. Steve Murray's video allows through Hermetic Law, and I stand witness, the awesome power of intent that this video brings to the Reiki understudy. *T.M.*

-I have been using your Reiki 1st , Healing Attunement, and Reiki 2nd videos for a few weeks now, with wonderful results. I feel the increase in my healing energy, more peace in my life, and greater comfort in my musculoskeletal system, where there has been some tension for several years. Thank you very much for your time, and God bless you for your healing videos. *C.E.J.*

Reiki Psychic Attunement

-Every time I go through the attunement I seem to feel a subtle sensation in my head, like a subtle shift in awareness. I haven't yet had any major experiences during or after the attunement like others have had, but it still seems to work. Over the course of several months along with other exercises, I have noticed that my intuition has gotten a lot better. Hard to explain, but my decisions are better and I notice a lot more of what's going on around me. Great value. *S.B.*

-I took the attunement several times with the crystal. All I can say is I do have greater awareness, and the awareness seems to be getting stronger. Of course I did not see visions or start to read people's minds, but for me it has been a subtle change of awareness which has helped me in my life. I have been working on my awareness for some time now, would it have happened without this attunement program, I don't know but -I'm sure it would have been slower to get where I am now. I think the attunement cleared me so I could process information more clearly and faster like Steve Murray said in the program. It really helped with my psychic awareness. *J. O.*

-The psychic program was very clear, very straight-forward. Although of course one can't be 100% certain what contributes to psychic "breakthroughs," especially when one meditates regularly with such improvements in mind, but I did have a noteworthy "success" the day after my first attunement. Contact with others who have crossed over has been normal for me since childhood, but this was the first time I "heard" several exact names of family members for an overseas client! So, I would say, this tape is worth a try. *B.J.*

-I bought both attunement programs Psychic and 1st Level. The Psychic Attunement has really opened up my psychic abilities on all levels, really can't say enough good things about it. It was beyond my expectations. **D.R.**

-This program worked for me. I was skeptical, but thought what the heck I spend more on readings and sometimes they are bad. I now have taken the attunement three times. I am now having dreams that are giving me information that has helped me in all aspects of my life. What's really funny is I never really remembered my dreams before, let alone giving me information. Also I am more intuitive now when it comes to daily life. **O.B.**

-It has really helped me in my psychic awareness and with my tarot readings. I do the attunement every week or so and each time I feel my awareness expanding and energy coming through. *R.W.*

-After the third time I took the attunement I was in an Internet chat room and a young woman that was very distressed over the death of her friend and her mother who died came in. I felt so sorry for her and wished with all my heart that I could help her. Suddenly these names and faces came to me and started communicating to me for her. I knew her mom and friends name, how they passed and there was a very long conversation. The young lady was happy and relieved to here from them and that was the day I began my work as a psychic medium. Since then I have bought every tape of Steve's I could find I don't have enough words to describe how wonderful this has been for me and how many people have been helped by my gifts being brought forth. **D.E.**

-I have taken the Psychic Attunement 3 times. In the third viewing of it, I saw three faces in the dead center of the Crystal, 2 male, and 1 female. I know this sounds weird, but I am telling you the faces were shifting in and out. One of the men was heavily bearded, as if he was of Indian descent, the other was Asian with a normal moustache, and the female had short Betty Boop like hair, but was Asian. I found this amazing and intense. I couldn't believe it! Thanks. **T.M.**

-I just was attuned through your healing and psychic videos. I was astounded at the feeling that I felt, which included feeling as though my body was vibrating, rocking and swirling. Thank you for creating such wonderful videos. Sincerely, **E.S.**

HOW TO ORDER VIDEOS, DVDS, & BOOKS

To buy any of the following Books, Videos, DVDs check with your local bookstore, or www.healingreiki.com or email bodymindheal@aol.com, or call 949-263-4676.

BOOKS BY STEVE MURRAY

Cancer Guided Imagery Program
For Radiation, Chemotherapy, Surgery,
And Recovery

Stop Eating Junk!
5 Minutes A Day-21 Day
Program

Reiki The Ultimate Guide
Learn Sacred Symbols and Attunements
Plus Reiki Secrets You Should Know

VIDEOS & DVDS BY STEVE MURRAY

Reiki Master Attunement
Become A Reiki Master

Reiki 1st Level Attunement
Give Healing Energy To
Yourself and Others

Reiki 2nd Level Attunement
Learn and Use the Reiki Sacred
Symbols

Reiki Psychic Attunement
Open and Expand Your Psychic
Abilities

Reiki Healing Attunement
Heal Emotional-Mental Physical-
Spiritual Issues

Preparing Mentally & Emotionally
For Cancer Surgery
A Guided Imagery Program

Preparing Mentally & Emotionally
For Cancer Surgery
A Guided Imagery Program

Preparing Mentally & Emotionally
For Cancer Chemotherapy
A Guided Imagery Program

Preparing Mentally & Emotionally
For Cancer Radiation
A Guided Imagery Program

Preparing Mentally &Emotionally
For Cancer Recovery
A Guided Imagery Program

Dissolving & Destroying Cancer Cells
A Guided Imagery Program
It!

Pain Relief Subliminal Program
Let Your Unconscious Mind Do

Fear & Stress Relief Subliminal
Program Let Your Unconscious
Mind Do The Work!

30-Day Subliminal Weight Loss
Program Let Your Unconscious
Mind Do The Work!

30-Day Subliminal Stop Smoking
Program Let Your Unconscious
Mind Do The Work!

VIDEOS BY BODY & MIND PRODUCTION

Learning To Read The Tarot
Intuitively

Learning To Read The Symbolism
Of The Tarot

About the Author

Steve Murray is an Usui Reiki Master, Tibetan and Karuna Reiki® Master. But one of his most powerful attunements came from the High Priest of the Essene Church, which made him an Essene Healer. The Essenes have been healers for over 2,000 years. Steve is also a Hypnotherapist and is a member of the National League of Medical Hypnotherapists and the National

ral books and has a series (17) of self-include topics on Reiki Attunements, weight loss, pain, fear, and stress relief programs soon will be available on private practice in Hypnotherapy and